Bob, MaryElle

Congratulations on your

Success in business and

as a family!

MW01493526

Tailored Wealth Management

Niall J. Gannon

Tailored Wealth Management

Exploring the Cause and Effect of Financial Success

palgrave
macmillan

Niall J. Gannon
The Gannon Group
St. Louis, MO, USA

Information contained herein has been obtained from sources considered to be reliable, but we do not guarantee their accuracy or completeness. The views expressed herein are those of the author and do not necessarily reflect the views of any organizations or entities in which the author is in employment or association. All opinions are subject to change without notice. Neither the information provided nor any opinion expressed constitutes a solicitation for the purchase or sale of any security. Past performance is no guarantee of future results.

ISBN 978-3-319-99779-7   ISBN 978-3-319-99780-3   (eBook)
https://doi.org/10.1007/978-3-319-99780-3

Library of Congress Control Number: 2018959110

© The Editor(s) (if applicable) and The Author(s), under exclusive licence to Springer International Publishing AG, part of Springer Nature 2019
This work is subject to copyright. All rights are solely and exclusively licensed by the Publisher, whether the whole or part of the material is concerned, specifically the rights of translation, reprinting, reuse of illustrations, recitation, broadcasting, reproduction on microfilms or in any other physical way, and transmission or information storage and retrieval, electronic adaptation, computer software, or by similar or dissimilar methodology now known or hereafter developed.
The use of general descriptive names, registered names, trademarks, service marks, etc. in this publication does not imply, even in the absence of a specific statement, that such names are exempt from the relevant protective laws and regulations and therefore free for general use.
The publisher, the authors and the editors are safe to assume that the advice and information in this book are believed to be true and accurate at the date of publication. Neither the publisher nor the authors or the editors give a warranty, express or implied, with respect to the material contained herein or for any errors or omissions that may have been made. The publisher remains neutral with regard to jurisdictional claims in published maps and institutional affiliations.

Cover illustration © Piriya Photography / Moment / Getty
Cover design by Tjaša Krivec

This Palgrave Macmillan imprint is published by the registered company Springer Nature Switzerland AG
The registered company address is: Gewerbestrasse 11, 6330 Cham, Switzerland

For Riley and Fiona

Acknowledgments

I offer gratitude to my editor, Tula Weis at Palgrave Macmillan, for believing in this project two years ago and for having the vision to help see it through. I am grateful to my developmental editor, Ellen Coleman, for not only completing her task with skill but also bringing new perspective to my views on the central topics of the book.

Thank you to the families whom I have come to know and serve over the past 25 years for believing in me and offering a classy example of how to lead a well-lived life.

Thank you to my wife, Gretchen, and my two daughters, Riley and Fiona, for enduring my loud and aggressive typing style that echoed through our home on many a day and night over the past year.

I remain grateful to Pat Kearns for offering me an internship at Shearson Lehman Brothers in 1991 that has led to such a fulfilling career. Thanks to Mark Bebensee from The Citadel and the late Sister Agnes Catherine Williams, OSU.

Thank you to colleagues and members of the CFA Institute for providing peer review on the Efficient Valuation Hypothesis, especially Brett Neubert, CFA. Overwhelming thanks to Scott Seibert, CFA, who co-authored the Efficient Valuation Hypothesis whitepaper and agreed to update valuation formulas, graphs, and tables for inclusion in this work. Thank you to the editors at Seeking Alpha, especially Mark Pentacoff, for highlighting our paper and agreeing to start a new debate in the financial services industry about the driver of portfolio returns over time.

Thanks to Charlotte Beyer, founder of the Institute for Private Investors and author of *Wealth Management Unwrapped* (Wiley, 2nd edition, 2017), for being so insistent that I continue to research ways to improve private investor outcomes.

Thank you to Dr. Aswath Damodaran, finance professor at New York University, for making his historical models available in an open-sourced format upon which we built our models.

Thank you to Charlie Henneman of the CFA Institute, whose invitation to address the delegates of the 2008 CFA Annual Conference led to my first book, and the models and refinements that grew from it.

Thank you to the members of Tiger 21, the Family Office Exchange, the Institute for Private Investors, Campden Wealth, and the Portfolio Management Institute for allowing me to share my work with their members. Thank you to His Holiness, Pope Francis, for helping me understand and act on ways to improve the human condition in the poorest parts of the world.

I maintain the ultimate level of respect and gratitude to Matt Rogers, Sarah Govreau, and Cindy Feaster for their dedication to the wealth management and family office profession.

Contents

List of Figures

List of Tables

List of Exhibits

Part I

The Landscape of Wealth Around the World

1

Introduction

Can a gas station attendant be wealthier than a gas company CEO? He can. As you read on, I'll name names and identify repeatable ways that the attendant did it.

Is the American dream and the prospect of wealth open to a 20-something worker who finds herself thousands of dollars in debt and surviving paycheck to paycheck? It is. Read on and I'll dissect how she changed her habits and her attitude toward money and we will follow her journey.

Can an individual investor outperform the "smart money" of American institutional investors by following a simple and understandable asset allocation and portfolio management framework? They can. I will share a few of the ways they may do it, including how to develop the ability to identify shifting risks and opportunities in the capital markets that can keep their plan on track.

Can you or I, an average person, implement a philanthropic plan that can eclipse the generosity of billionaires like Bill Gates who have taken the Giving Pledge? We can. I will talk about ways to make this very thing happen while allowing our own savings and retirement planning to remain focused.

Can the dollars we spend redistribute wealth to other members of society in a repeatable and sustainable way? Yes, without question they can. I will explain how to make it happen.

I've chosen to attack these questions, do the research, and share the results because I believe the time is right to do so. While the word "wealth" has come to mean abundance for some, it has become a bad word in too many corners of our society and throughout the world. When the roadmap to wealth and happiness is painted over with failure or jealousy we deny ourselves and our neighbors the unalienable right to pursue and, more important, to achieve happiness.

© The Author(s) 2019
N. J. Gannon, *Tailored Wealth Management*,
https://doi.org/10.1007/978-3-319-99780-3_1

Tailored Wealth Management will address three pillars of wealth:

- Identifying and building it
- Managing it
- Deploying it

Part I: The Landscape of Wealth around the World will provide you with the facts that will help you develop a more informed view of wealth, not only as it relates to you, but also how it relates to your neighbor or a family who lives halfway around the world. It will inspire you to acknowledge the strengths and advantages that are unique to where you find yourself in life and fortify you with stories of people just like you who are breaking down the barriers to wealth in their own lives. You'll do well to understand and adapt their habits and make them your own.

Too often, when we think about wealth, we think of the people higher up on the net worth ladder. In this book, I will shine a bright light on the wealth ladder, let you know where you stand compared with the other seven billion people on the globe, and let you decide for yourself whether the road to wealth, abundance, and happiness are open to you and your family.

Wealth management, in and of itself, should not be complicated. But for all too many individual and institutional investors it has become complicated. That has led to failure and it is imperative that investors take inventory of the lessons learned from the last quarter century not only to not repeat them, but so that the new generation of investors who haven't yet made a single mistake may learn from them. Specifically, academic studies from the twentieth century have become twisted into myths on Wall Street. We will, and we must, break them down for what they are and what they are not. To that end, I will share a new way of looking at forward portfolio forecasting that I believe is superior to the models that have left Americans with trillions of dollars of unfunded pension plans and retirement accounts.

The third pillar of wealth is redistribution and it would be a lie to call it by any other name. Every dollar we have ever saved, inherited, won, found, or earned will eventually pass on or, as I think of it, compost into the soil of another person or entity. Those who have been successful at the first two pillars of wealth would do well to tighten their focus on how, who, and when to redistribute their money lest that decision be made by someone else after they die. When your cup runneth over, the prudent wealthy person will ensure that not a drop is spilled on the ground so that all of it reaches its intended recipient.

Cause and effect is a theme that runs throughout *Tailored Wealth Management*. If I identify an effect, I owe it to you (to the best of my ability) to identify the cause that brought that effect into being. Challenge me, readers, if I have gotten it wrong. The people to whom you'll be introduced in Chap. 2 are not outliers. They are regular people who have shown that wealth and happiness is achievable. The Efficient Valuation Hypothesis, the bedrock of Part II, is my rebuttal to the roulette wheel of Wall Street that many investors believe is their only option. In Part III, I will discuss spending your money, passing it on to your family, and giving it away to strangers. It is debatable whether building wealth or redistributing wealth is more fun, but the sharing habits of those who have done both well should leave you stronger than you were before you learned their stories.

I have given you my best with this work. Give yourself and your family your best once you finish the book.

2

Average Americans: Stories of "Ordinary" Success

In *Investing Strategies*, I shared the story of Dennis and Judy Jones who turned their life savings of $100,000 into a $3.6 billion company by the time they rang the closing bell of the New York Stock Exchange on August 30, 2000. The Jones' tale of success, which brought them from the trailer they lived in as newlyweds to the upper echelons of wealth, is impressive; in fact, it is so spectacular, to bring us down to earth, I feel I should tell you a few stories about regular folks who achieved a more moderate success and how they did it.

Before I get to these tales of ordinary *financial* success, I want to share two observations that speak to the causes of success in young people and its effect on them. The first is a young man named Trevor Kates, who plays the piano very well. My daughter Fiona's piano teacher is Kiley Kozel, who enjoys hosting periodic recitals during which her students get to show off their current work. At one particular recital her student Trevor played with incredible precision, passion, and artistry. It reminded me of Geoffrey Rush in the movie *Shine* as he slayed Rachmaninoff's "Concerto Number 3," only Trevor was just 11 years old! When he completed the piece, around the auditorium, I heard "He's simply gifted," echoing throughout the audience. At the conclusion of the recital, Kiley gave out awards to the children based on the number of minutes they practiced the piano that month. After presenting the awards for 60 minutes, 120 minutes, and 500 minutes, it was Trevor's turn. He had practiced for 27 hours and 21 minutes that month. Trevor may indeed be "gifted," but the *cause* of his success no doubt came, at least in part, from the amount of work he put into his art; the *effect* of all that effort was the polished gem that resulted.

Another example of effort leading to results came on the day my other daughter, Riley, graduated from high school. Of the top five members of the

© The Author(s) 2019
N. J. Gannon, *Tailored Wealth Management*,
https://doi.org/10.1007/978-3-319-99780-3_2

graduating class (as measured by cumulative grade point average), two received the perfect attendance award for never having missed a day of school for all four years. Cause and effect anyone?

And now, let's return to our average Americans.

The Cause, the Money Habit; the Effect, a Nest Egg

My first example is of a young adult, JP Livingston, who retired at the age of 28 with $2.2 million in the bank. Today, JP is the author of a financial blog called www.themoneyhabit.org. According to JP, both of her parents were raised in humble conditions; in fact, her father grew up with eight people living in a one-room apartment. To make ends meet, the family had to be frugal. Her father graduated from college, and her mother worked as a secretary after her children were old enough to go to school.

Early on, they knew that if JP wanted to attend college, she would have to work hard to get good grades and scholarships, which she did. In fact, she earned enough merit-based scholarships to attend UCLA on a full ride, but JP aimed for and eventually attended Harvard, which meant she had to shoulder some of the tuition through loans. To minimize the cost of her Harvard degree, JP realized that by graduating in three years instead of four, she would save over $50,000. She also realized that if she actually HAD $50,000 and wisely invested it, it could grow handsomely over the next ten years. Of course, she didn't have a nest egg at the time, but this thought led her to study the impact of financial decisions made early in one's life or career.

Her initial plan was to graduate and start her own business, but an investment bank recruiter on campus offered her a job after graduation in 2009 with a starting salary of $60,000. While the thought of being her own boss sounded great, the stability and experience that she could get working at a top-tier Wall Street firm was obviously the wise choice. Just as she understood she could minimize her college costs by graduating early, JP understood that the chance to make a bonus of up to $40,000 would be driven by hard work and achieving results. She did both, earned the bonus and received a six-figure paycheck right out of the gate.

As much as she enjoyed her job, JP's long-term goal was to become a writer—although not a starving one. To achieve her dream, she would need to be wealthy enough not to have to work a traditional 50- to 60-hour-per-week job; essentially she would have to retire at an early age. To achieve this she maintained a maniacal dedication to her job and continued practicing the frugality taught to her by her parents and grandparents. It took her eight years to achieve the "wealth" that would allow her to take the step of becoming a self-employed writer. For JP Livingston, the way to achieve wealth can be summed up in two simple equations:

$$Income - Expenses = Savings$$
$$Savings + Growth\ Rate - Taxes = Nest\ Egg$$

In her blog, JP explains that out of the $60,000 gross pay (excluding bonus) she decided she could spend $24,000 after tax on living expenses and, therefore, could save the rest (including the bonus). Although on her salary she could have lived in a relatively trendy part of Manhattan, she opted for a studio outside of the city where her rent was $1100 per month. And that's how over eight years she built her $2.2 million nest egg.

Today, JP is married. Her husband is still employed. Together, they now spend $32,500 per person per year, a total of $65,000 per year. That is a 35% increase in their standard of living assuming that together they had spent $24,000 (per person) per year, or $48,000 per year, as JP was doing when she was single.

JP and her husband know that their annual living expenses of $65,000 could easily be covered by a 2.9% draw from their $2.2 million portfolio, but they know that taking 2.9% from their portfolio would rob it of the compounding effect on those funds. Instead, they choose to allow the portfolio to grow and cover expenses out of her husband's salary. Savings and investing are not a thing of the past for this couple because they wish to continue to grow their net worth so that in the future they can have greater flexibility about how they spend their free time. They have set the trajectory of how and when they wish to enjoy such things as leisure activities and fancy homes in smaller steps than their peers.

Living around New York City, as this young couple now does, demands that as they continue their journey they maintain and hone the discipline that built their portfolio. They live in a 325-square-foot apartment on the fifth floor of a walkup. JP jokes that the floors are so slanted that if you drop a marble, it will make its way to the wall by the force of gravity. Groceries come from neighborhood grocers in Chinatown or Trader Joe's; furniture is purchased off Craigslist. Their rather modest lifestyle is a choice that makes them smile.

Today, we're all bombarded with messages telling us that to be happy we need more and more things, and that families need two incomes just to "get by." JP doesn't buy into that thinking. Sure, you might be thinking; it is easy for her to say now that she has a few million in the bank, but don't forget she made a conscious choice NOT to do certain things in order to be able to do what she does. Clearly JP and her husband have painstakingly assessed the landmines that take wealth creation off track and have prioritized accordingly. We will discuss "wealth robbers" in Chap. 5.

JP Livingston has the comfort of knowing she can rejoin the investment bank at any time she chooses. If she does, she might continue to climb the corporate ladder and begin another decade of saving and wealth creation that will be orders of magnitude greater than what she accomplished in the first decade of her career. On the other hand, she may decide not to go back to work.

My point in recounting JP's story is that this young woman performed the financial equivalent of Babe Ruth's pointing the bat to the spot in the bleachers where he would hit the winning home run in a 1932 World Series game. JP, playing her own game, called a terrific shot in the world series of her life.

The Cause, Downsizing, and Reprioritizing; the Effect, Quitting Debt, and the Rat Race

Jenna Spesard, 32, made a dramatic change in her lifestyle in order to immediately begin living her new brand of personal success and happiness. Armed with a graduate degree and working in Hollywood toward a career in screen writing, Ms. Spesard decided she had enough of the daily treadmill in which her fellow "ladder climbers" were engaged. She looked at the money she paid in rent, the cost of dressing fashionably, and turned her eye toward a more freestyle existence that would allow her to write and travel the world. She quit her job and built (along with her partner at the time) a 165-square-foot house on wheels in which she has now traveled over 25,000 miles. Her story, which is chronicled on her blog tinyhousegiantjourney.com, is the base for her livelihood in which she estimates her income at $52,000 to $62,000. The majority of her income comes from views on her YouTube channel. I caught up with Ms. Spesard one morning after she traveled from the East Coast to Seattle. I was interested in her view of the cause and effect that would come from making such a dramatic lifestyle change. In short, she added up what she was spending on wants versus needs, redefined what a need was to her, and set out to reduce her indebtedness left over from her graduate degree, which was about $30,000 at the time. Today, her total debt is below $9000 and she is on track to be debt free by year end 2019.

I asked Jenna if she would switch places with a random billionaire, which of course would come with the mansion, the yacht, the jet, and the army of household staff. Her answer was a definitive negative. "You aren't your things," she replied. "Things" that don't have emotional value or fulfill a practical need create clutter and chaos. If she were to be fortunate enough to have a robust net worth, it would have to be the engine to drive a philanthropic or humanitarian purpose. Jenna advises young people to look at the bigger picture, insisting that the way we spend our time is far more important than the amount we have in the bank. Ms. Spesard doesn't eschew money or wealth; she simply states that people who live in the tiny house movement are "turning the American dream on its head." Her story was refreshing to me, especially when thinking of the black hole we often hear about regarding under-funded pensions and below-target savings rates for the next few generations of retirees.

Jenna will, however, continue to grow her "nest egg" as she hopes to start a family one day who won't be raised in a tiny house; they will be raised in a modest house. Jenna's success shines a bright light on the darkness many young people perceive about "getting ahead." She doesn't worry about the person to her left or to her right. Jenna Spesard is running her own race.

The Cause, Frugality and Investing Wisely; the Effect, the Joy of Giving

The story of Ronald Reade (janitor and gas station attendant) is fascinating, not just because he secretly amassed millions and not just because his goal was to give it all away to his community instead of spending it on himself. It is fascinating because it is a wonderfully executed plan which marries cause and effect to a specific goal in life. Ron's success as a saver and investor became known only months after his death when his estate awarded a $6 million gift to his town's local hospital and library and $2 million to his caregivers, friends, and family. His obituary on Legacy.com is a fun read, especially because there is no mention of his most notable success, which was as an investor. I wonder how the attendance at his funeral would have changed if it did.

The obituary, published on June 5, 2014, in the *Brattleboro Reformer*, chronicled the well-lived life of a World War II veteran. Reade died at the age of 92. As a graduate of Brattleboro High School, Ron joined the US Army and served as a military policeman, stationed in Italy. He was known as an avid outdoorsman; chopping wood brought him particular joy. After returning from overseas, Ron worked as a gas station attendant. Later in life, he married Barbara March who predeceased him by 44 years. His final employment was as the janitor at the JC Penney. He was buried at Meeting House Hill Cemetery. Humbly, he requested that any memorials should be made to the Dummerston Historical Society in Dummerston, Vermont.

When the announcement of Ron's gift to the library and the hospital finally came, countless newspapers, periodicals, and bloggers rushed to break the news of what this simple man was able to accomplish over his lifetime. Not surprisingly, Ron was frugal. Like JP Livingston, he saved more than he spent. He invested wisely, leaving a stack of 95 stock certificates in his safe deposit box. In the portfolio, blue-chip heavyweights[1] were well represented along with a handful of certificates in companies that were now worthless. Ron understood the concept of long-term investments. He understood that dividends were a function of those businesses' profits. He understood that in a diversified portfolio, some of what you thought were your best ideas will be worthless. He understood that day-trading was likely to be less profitable than diligently acquiring quality companies and holding them for a long period of time.

Unlike others who have amassed wealth, Mr. Reade uniquely apparently lacked the stomach to deal with his wealth publicly. He didn't want people to see him as "rich" or even as generous. He spent those 92 years, I would suspect, balancing the "fun" that comes from successful investing and the personal drive that committed him to doing something spectacular for his community. We will never know what motivated him. If the Dummerston Historical Society, Vermont, is open to suggestions, I hope they emphasize the generosity he displayed as a veteran and as a member of his community and not focus on the fact that he was a real-life American tycoon.

The Cause, Modest Expectations; the Effect, Living Life to Its Fullest

My next example of "ordinary" success has to be pseudonymous. I'll call him Ike. He is a deceased friend whose privacy I will respect. I met Ike in 1994 after cold-calling him one evening. It was the kind of call that makes my job worthwhile. It was a tad before 9 p.m. one weeknight when Ike told me, "I am a doctor. I am divorced. I lost a lot of money in tax partnerships in the 80s.

---

[1] www.wsj.com, "Route to an $8 million portfolio started with frugal living," March 19, 2015.

The divorce cleaned me out. I am remarried now, have nearly $1 million saved up in a basket of no-load mutual funds and I have no idea what the hell I am doing."

He asked me if we could meet at his office at 7 the next morning to see if I might be what he was looking for. Simply put, he told me, "Niall, I want to retire soon, buy a home in Florida for cash, live off the interest from my portfolio and enjoy the remaining years of my life. You tell me what I can afford and what kind of budget will work and we will do that." Ike's goal was simple, his expectations were humble, and I became a big fan of him, both as an investor and as a man who wanted to live well.

Every Christmas for the next 20 years, a box of beautiful Florida citrus would arrive at my door from Ike and his wife. He died a couple of years ago, peacefully. His wife still lives in their condo (with no mortgage), has a car with no payments, and adjusts her budget to maximize her enjoyment of life. In those two decades they owned a boat, ate a lot of grouper, joined a Japanese flower arranging club, and laughed a lot. One of Ike's goals was to ensure that his bride wouldn't have to worry about money after he died. Even though she didn't enjoy having annual reviews with her financial advisor she would listen in and capture the essence of the conversation.

At every turn, Ike had the opportunity to buy a new Cadillac instead of a used one. Ike and his wife could have taken their cruises with a balcony room instead of an interior one. They could have bought a big house instead of a more humble one. They could have gone out to dinner more often than they ate at home. They could have hired a financial advisor that buried the needle in risk, but they opted for a more conservative approach. As I came to know Ike and his wife better, it was clear that they had command over the difference between "wants" and "needs" as well as the understanding to plan for a long, healthy life. Ike was wealthy, and I sure am grateful that he gave me a chance to be a part of his life.

The Cause, Total Commitment and Hard Work; the Effect, Reaching Your Goal

Mike is an admirable young person I came to admire whom I met one evening in the mid-1990s, while enjoying the all-you-can-eat buffet at our local Pizza Hut. He intrigued me because he was "all in" on being the best busboy ever. Although the restaurant had a self-service soda fountain, Mike raced between tables refilling customers' half-full glasses. I watched him telling jokes to one table of senior citizens, who laughed appreciatively. At our table, he asked if we had a favorite type of pizza that was not on the buffet that night and offered to request it from the kitchen. I forget whether the buffet was $4, $5, or $6 but I remember feeling that I was getting more than I paid for.

I was new in the brokerage business at that time and was looking for someone who could cold-call prospective clients with me at night and on weekends. I gave him my office number which he called promptly at 8 the following Monday morning. I hired Mike, and we worked together when his schedule allowed for the next year. I lost Mike when he got a better offer (good for him) from the St. Louis Vipers Roller Hockey team, which was looking for a new cameraman. I was happy for him and wished him well.

Every Christmas since then, I receive a card with a short note from Mike telling me how he is doing. After the roller hockey team folded, he got a job driving a bakery truck in St. Louis. I believe he reported to the job every morning at 2 and his paycheck reflected these inconvenient hours. Mike took every route he could, kept his expenses low, and saved a lot of his wages. After a few years, Mike bought a bakery delivery truck and began soliciting orders directly from various bakeries to make deliveries to customers around town. A few years later, now with a nicely established route, customer list, and well-maintained truck, someone approached him to sell the business and the price was right. Mike got married, bought a house, had a son, and his LinkedIn profile indicates he is now a territory sales manager at a major national baked goods company. Mike is wealthy.

How "Ordinary" Becomes Extraordinary

The lives highlighted above are not outliers. They did not rely on winning the lottery, becoming a paper millionaire at the IPO of a hot tech company, inheriting a bundle, or any other extraordinary event. They achieved wealth through hard work and good planning. Each of these individuals mastered the art of living below their means, a robust habit of saving and investing, an admirable work ethic, and, in a few cases such as in Mike and Ike's, a touch of humility.

I am speaking most directly now to you, the young adult who is either finishing or finished with college. I am speaking to that young woman or man who has enlisted in the navy as a single person and is wondering what you will do with your regular pay, sea pay, nuclear or hazardous duty pay while living on a ship or submarine with nowhere to spend it. It is absolutely your right to buy the convertible and eat fine sushi right out of the gate, but for those of you who wonder whether you will be a slave to your job your entire life: think again. You haven't made any mistakes yet with the money you are set to earn. You haven't developed any bad habits that will rob you of excess capital. You have every right and opportunity to adopt the traits exemplified by these examples of ordinary success OR you may decide to aim to become one of the Forbes 400 yourself. While making the Forbes list isn't the path I walk, it may be yours. If becoming Jeff Bezos sounds too far-fetched, ask yourself if you could live like JP, Like Jenna, like Ron Reade, like Ike, or like Mike. It's your race, no one else's.

My mission in this and subsequent chapters is to understand the habits that make people wealthy. I hope to motivate you and help you envision a lifestyle and work backward from that goal to develop a plan that will make it a reality. Many people who wish to become wealthy but do not were unwilling to undertake certain "less fun" behaviors, such as delaying gratification, working harder than the guy in the next cube, and saving instead of spending in the moment.

These stories of ordinary success highlight the fact that any healthy individual can practice these traits, but the earlier a person begins, the more likely their success. These behaviors have less of an impact on older people, who have less time available to them to effect a meaningful change. Young people, on the other hand, have no excuse not to practice these traits if they aspire to wealth; if they don't they must accept that they have made a personal choice not to achieve it.

Keep these stories in mind as inspiration as you pursue your goals, but also seek out people in your life who display the traits of a wealthy person; that is, they carry themselves as if they have it good in life. Their means are greater than their needs. They work hard and express confidence that there is a path forward for them, should they choose to take it. They live free of jealousy. JP, Jenna, Ron, Ike, and Mike are four people whose stories I wanted to share but there are countless others. I have seen happy, wealthy people who work the cash register at Walgreens. I have seen happy school teachers who enjoy moonlighting a few hours for Uber so they can buy fun things and have interesting experiences. I have seen people who quit six-figure, high-potential careers to take significant pay cuts so they could work in the non-profit sector. I have seen vibrant, young school teachers who work at an inner city Catholic school knowing full well that they could meaningfully increase their wages by taking a job in a more affluent public school district. They choose not to do so because they know the parents of their young students are paying all they can afford and feel called to pass solid knowledge and skills so that their students may begin (hopefully) a better life than their parent(s) experienced.

There are "wealthy" people in your life. Study them and see if you can adopt a few of their admirable traits.

3

Wealth: How Much Do You Need; How Much Is Enough

In 2017, an entry-level police officer in the United States earned an annual wage of $44,160, according to payscale.com.[1] If she began the job at age 20, works until age 65, and receives a 3% raise every year, that officer will retire with an annual income of $167,000 and have earned $4.2 million in cumulative wages over her career. If she achieves the rank of sergeant after ten years on the job, it will bump her career earnings to $5.6 million. If she is promoted to lieutenant after 20 years, her cumulative wages rise to $6.86 million.

I suspect that many of you are surprised that a median-level income such as this police officer's could produce a multiple seven-figure wage opportunity. Yet many people, out of necessity or out of habit live from paycheck to paycheck or spend all they earn, lose out on or diminish the opportunity for savings and wealth creation. This is true despite the fact that except for the obligation to pay taxes, many young people have full discretion over how and when our money is spent, saved, or gifted.

According to globalrichlist.com, the median annual wage in 2017 for a global worker was $1400 per year. This means that of the seven billion of the world's inhabitants, half make more and half make less than this amount. If the median wage earner earns $1400 per year, how does this compare to those living at or below the poverty line in the United States? The US Department of Health and Human Services guidelines place the federal poverty line for a family of four in 2017 at $24,600 (regardless of the number of wage earners in the family). But numbers alone don't tell the whole story. Surely, a newly

---

[1] http://www.payscale.com/research/U.S./Job=Police_Officer/Salary/9d8677f9/Entry-Level.

© The Author(s) 2019
N. J. Gannon, *Tailored Wealth Management*,
https://doi.org/10.1007/978-3-319-99780-3_3

discharged sergeant in the US Army who received an annual wage of $37,152 and has no dependents has a markedly different view of wealth than a single teacher earning the same wage, living with two young children, and supporting an aging parent. My objective in this chapter is not to form or change your view on the issues of inequality or a living wage; it is to simply inform and provide some perspective about wealth that might help readers, especially to young people who have not made any significant financial mistakes.

According to the Global Rich List calculator, this income (the US poverty line) actually falls in the top 2.09% of wage earners globally. The *median* US family income is $59,039, an amount that puts that family in the top 1% of global wage earners. These numbers may surprise you. However, Americans represent only 4% of the world's population, so it is not that unbelievable that our definition of poverty is nearly 20 times the wages of the average global worker.

My purpose in sharing this information is not to minimize the struggles of any one group, but simply to provide perspective and to suggest that Americans would do well to view wealth and income globally rather than nationally or regionally. I suggest you visit globalrichlist.com, input your country and income, and see where you rank among the world's inhabitants. It can be an enlightening exercise. Admittedly, this number by itself is a bit simplistic. Variations in cost of living, healthcare, and other necessities have to be added to the equation, but the facts will likely surprise you and, I hope, spark your curiosity and make you think about your relationship to wealth in a way that may help you in the journey that follows as you read this book. At the very least it should make those of you living in developed countries realize that you are or have a reasonable opportunity to be or become wealthy.[2]

Real People; Real Measures of Wealth

Thinking about wealth and poverty globally made me think about people I have met—members of the Forbes 400—who, despite their vast wealth, do not *feel* wealthy. How is that possible? Even more curious to me is that I have encountered many members of this group and their extended families, who feel that wealth has destroyed their lives, relationships, and happiness. Many of you probably read about the suicide of a New York hedge fund manager who in 2016 jumped to his death despite having a net worth of

---

[2] Speaking for myself, personally and as an advisor, this exercise and these statistics made me think anew about where to effectively direct philanthropy, and led me to include in my own plan helping those outside the United States as well as continuing to give to those local organizations that do so much good at home.

over $70 million because he built a lifestyle for his family that he felt he could no longer sustain.

Compare this to Ronald Reade (Chap. 2), who secretly amassed an $8 million fortune over his lifetime by living simply, saving wisely, and investing shrewdly. Indeed, no one knew of his wealth until his death only at 92, when his local hospital and library received a combined $6 million bequest. We can confidently say that Ron Reade, the Vermont janitor and gas station attendant, was wealthier than the extravagant New York hedge fund manager or than the infamous Ken Lay, the gas company CEO, who became the disgraced face of the Enron Corporation accounting fraud. I believe that, if today your bank account is robust, you, too, can adopt the proper attitude and habits of responsible wealth management, and that those who have not yet reached that level can also become wealthy, just as Ron Reade did, by wisely choosing where you spend, how much you save, how wisely you invest, and how effectively you return it to society or your family by the time of your death.

Wealth has many measures; here's an example of wealth on a different scale. John was a worker at a Kenyan safari tent camp. I met him several years ago during a mission trip. John's job was to walk guests from the dining tent back to their sleeping tents and deal with any animals from an elephant or a curious warthog they encountered along the way. John's wages, about $850 per year, were in the lower half of the global average. While as part of his remuneration John was given a tent to sleep in and food to eat, a more important side benefit was that there was literally no place for him to spend money. This very quickly taught him the concept of savings and economic upward mobility.

John was a fascinating, joyful man, who would stop during the day to peer through his binoculars and describe the beauty of the bird or animal within its sights. Since we were at the camp only three nights, our time together was brief but long enough for me to learn more about where he wished to go in his life. At night, John would study by candlelight; he was determined to get his driver/chauffer license and then ultimately to gain certification as a wildlife guide or safari driver. If he could achieve this goal and find a job, his wages (he estimated) would be $1800 to $2300 per year and he would have the opportunity to earn generous tips from American, Asian, and European tourists. When I asked him what his plans were for the additional income he would receive from the new job, he answered, "To send my younger sisters to a private school—a chance that I never had."

As I see it, John was wealthy. What I found incredible to fathom, as I thought about it on the flight home, was the fact that if John succeeded in attaining his safari guide job, his income would nearly triple, which would take him from the bottom half of global wage earners into the top. This may not be the type of upward economic mobility we speak of in the developed world, but it would be very significant to John and his family.

John envisioned a path that would remarkably change his life, and, in doing so, he would also provide opportunities for his sisters who would benefit from the private education they would receive. That's what caused John's desire for upward mobility. If John hadn't believed that this was possible, he wouldn't have spent those evenings studying. John understood that learning a new and more valued skill would lead to a more highly paid profession.

Relative Definitions of Wealth

"How much is enough?" Throughout my career, this has been the most difficult question to answer for families. For the lucky ones, the sale of their business occurs late in their career, in their mid-50s or 60s. At that point, they have seen friends and colleagues die and grandchildren born, and so the decision to hang up their cleats concurrent with the sale of their business is an easy one.

For inheritors of wealth, the question of "how much is enough" can be more difficult. There are rightfully many grateful and content inheritors of wealth. Those who fit this description recognize that they are living an enormously privileged life. Others, who may have less pleasant memories of the wealth creator, are able to segregate those feelings and appreciate the fact that they are living the life they do because of what they received.

Not all inheritors of wealth display a level of gratitude and contentment. Ironically, perceptions of wealth can be driven by the idea of *inequality*. In the same way that members (low on the list) of the Forbes 400 can be jealous of #1, it is not uncommon for inheritors of wealth to be jealous of one another. If son number one has $100 million and passes that on to his only daughter, she may receive roughly $50 million net of estate taxes and claims against the estate. If son number two has four daughters, their $50 million will be split four ways, or $12.5 million each. While equality was achieved at the second generation, the wealth transfer at the third left one cousin four times wealthier than the others. Certainly, it is not the fault of the only child, but jealousy over what the other cousin or uncle received can consume some heirs to so great a degree that they will never feel wealthy. This is an unpleasant example of the glass half-empty syndrome. Inheritors who fall victim to this thinking worry more about what everybody else (in their family) has instead of focusing on enjoying what they have.

In the course of my career, I have seen elaborate plans concocted in an attempt to be "fair" and equitable, but, in the end, I have come to accept that while equality can be reached at a moment in time, it is impossible to achieve *over* time. The proof of this can be seen in the story of two brothers who sold an equal stake in a Midwestern manufacturing operation in the early 2000s. Each received approximately $7 million in pre-tax proceeds. Nearly two decades have now passed. The first brother is down to about $4 million in assets plus the value of his home. Although he was young at the time of the sale, he never gained permanent employment, but instead lived off the proceeds of his bank account. The second brother now has over $14 million in assets. Like his brother, at the time of the sale, he purchased a new home, but he also sought out and obtained a job with a multiple six-figure compensation plan. He wisely invested the capital from the sale of the business so that he could slow down in his mid- to late 50s. While perfect wealth equality was achieved at the time of the sale of the business, a twofold level of inequality now exists between the two brothers. What caused this disparity and its effect is evident.

In the same way that equality can be nearly impossible to achieve among the heirs of a wealthy family, it is similarly difficult (despite very good intentions) to achieve and maintain equality among members of society. As a result, it is not uncommon for people with less to be jealous of those with more, no matter how much money they have.

Jealousy of someone further up the wealth ladder is futile. Not only does jealousy rob the brain of the creative energy needed to build personal wealth, but it tends to continue even when someone has achieved wealth. That's because the person remains fixated on the distance between him and the next guy. And there is always a "next guy" who is richer or more powerful than you are. In the yachting industry it is called "tenfootitis." That is to say, moments after a proud owner pulls his 150-foot yacht into the harbor in St. Barth, another boat 160 feet in length is right behind him. That is silly, isn't it?

I enjoy spending leisure time along the coast of South Carolina. There, it seems, "tenfootitis" has not affected boat owners the way it has in St. Barth, St. Tropez, or Monte Carlo. What could cause the difference? Let me try to explain: Along the creeks, rivers, and intra-coastal waterway around Charleston nearly everybody owns a boat or knows somebody who owns a boat. On a nice Saturday morning in June, with the winds calm and expected temperatures in the mid-80s the boat ramps are all abuzz. Once the boats are launched and begin their dance of cutting across the waterways, a fun exercise begins: you watch people enjoy the day as you pass them or they pass you. You will see some beautiful large motor yachts and sailboats. There will be multimillion-dollar Hatteras sport fishers, zooming their way to the coastal shelf going after mahi-mahi, grouper, or tilefish.

But what you will see most is regular people with modest boats and they look really happy. It is impossible not to smile when you pass a camouflage-painted johnboat, skippered by a sunglass-wearing 20-something steering the boat with his handled outboard motor. On the bow of the boat, there's usually a dog. Next to the skipper there might be a bikini-wearing passenger and one or two friends to round out the group. There might be a cooler with sandwiches, beer, and some frozen Snickers bars and there can be no doubt that this crew will hit the day hard. I cannot say for sure that jealousy never crosses the mind of other skippers. What I can say? I am happy to be in *my* boat and could not care less about what the next guy is doing in his boat. If you are a boater, the next time you find yourself on the water and you spot a modest vessel with folks in search of a good time, ask yourself if they are having as good a day as you or anyone else on the water that day. If they are, they are wealthy in that moment, content with what they have and enjoying it to the very fullest. Take note of the wisdom emanating from that modest vessel.

I am always amazed to hear stories of people with $5 or $10 million in the bank who feel like they have been "screwed" in life when, at the same time, someone living across the globe like John believes he will be wealthy with an annual income of $2000 per year. Having said that, my goal in this chapter is not to preach, scold, or finger wag, but to simply present the numbers in a way that you can develop an informed view of wealth for yourself.

Wealth and Happiness

Several attempts have been made at studying the income or net worth necessary for happiness. These studies warrant consideration not because they agree on a specific number, but because they attempt to measure how much is necessary to truly remove certain worries from an individual's life. For starters, imagine what it would be like if you could live your life completely free of worry about a retirement nest egg or your ability to pay for your children's college education. Removing these two worries from a family can be a financial goal in and of itself, and can serve as a wonderful template for an older wealth creator considering how much and when to gift assets to his extended family.

Daniel Kahneman and Angus Deaton, respectively 2002 and 2015 winners of the Nobel Memorial Prize in Economic Sciences, have studied the relationship between income and happiness, and reported their findings in a whitepaper in the *Proceedings of the National Academy of Sciences*.[3] In it they suggest

---

[3] Kahneman D, Deaton A. High income improves evaluation of life but not emotional well-being. *Proceedings of the National Academy of Sciences of the United States of America*. 2010; 107 (38):16489–16493. https://doi.org/10.1073/pnas.1011492107.

that happiness does increase with additional income, but that no further progress in emotional well-being is observed above an annual income of $75,000. The paper, which was based on an analysis of the 1000 US residents conducted by the Gallup Organization in the Gallup-Healthways Well-Being Index, deserves consideration by anyone asking the question, "How much is enough?"

According to data released by the Social Security Administration at www. socialsecurity.gov, the average social security benefit awarded to an individual who applied for benefits was $1413 per month or $16,956 annually (March 2018). A married retired couple who both paid into the social security system during their wage-earning years (assuming equal benefit) would receive $33,912 annually. This amount, if combined with a 4.5% distribution rate from a $1 million nest egg, could achieve gross income of $78,912. Of course, inflation and regional adjustments are needed to distill this example into a real-life scenario for a couple, but it is indeed encouraging that the young police officer in our earlier example has within her reach the ability to build a retirement income as defined by Kahneman and Deaton capable of providing comfort and happiness.

Pessimists may dismiss these findings, wondering where that leaves those who make less than the police officer, or those whose fortunes were dashed by the loss of a wage-earning spouse early in life, or once one of the recipients dies, among other understandable exceptions to this general rule. Optimists will point to our frugal janitor who never received a salary anywhere close to $75,000 per year and say that happiness is more than just a number. While Mr. Reade's wages as a gas station attendant or janitor must have put him in the bottom quartile of US wage earners, the $8 million portfolio he amassed through shrewd investing and robust saving *could* have provided him with an annual income of $320,000 ($8 million times 4%). Mr. Reade didn't want, or need, $320,000. Apparently, his happiness came from saving for a different goal, only made public when the town newspaper announced his posthumous gift to the community.

Is $1 million in your 401k enough to make you happy? How about $5 million? The real-life examples used in this chapter were chosen to illustrate how those at various points on the wealth and income scale were able not only to pursue but find happiness. To all young people in the developed economies of America, Europe, and Asia, I would say, there is no barrier to your path to wealth. Study the raw materials of successful savers and investors, understand what creates financial success and what its effects are, and ignore what the man or woman next to you is doing. They are following their path. You should follow yours.

4

The Growth of American Wealth: Its Impact on the Average Household Compared with the Forbes 400

American households and non-profit organizations had a total net worth of nearly $100 trillion in net assets (after deducting $15.4 trillion in total liabilities including home mortgages) at year end 2017.[1] Since the Federal Reserve's report combines household and non-profit net worth, it should be noted that non-profit organizations (including family foundations) represent approximately 5% of the $100 trillion, a number that represents 36% of all global wealth—$280 trillion—as reported by the Credit Suisse Research Institute.

While much has been written about the stagnating or under-performing wealth of the average family, viewing *total* household wealth paints a brighter picture than viewing any sub-component of society. When we studied the progress of US household wealth back to 1952, the annualized growth rate was 6.82%. This number may at first seem high so before we go further, let's take a deeper dive into the sometimes-overlooked components of wealth, as used in the Fed's report.

When investors calculate their net worth, they normally include their liquid bank, security, and retirement accounts along with the value of real estate and household items less any liabilities. US households hold $27.4 trillion worth of real estate against which they owe $10 trillion in home mortgage debt. Netting the two puts average home equity at 63.6% of the average home's value.

What investors often do not include in their calculations are assets such as life insurance reserves and future pension benefits. That's because most people

---

[1] Federal Reserve of the United States, Financial Accounts of the United States, Table R.101, page 141, Third Quarter 2017.

© The Author(s) 2019
N. J. Gannon, *Tailored Wealth Management*,
https://doi.org/10.1007/978-3-319-99780-3_4

view their pension as income not as an asset and life insurance as something that goes to their heirs and, therefore, not an asset. For the married couple who earned the average monthly social security benefit, their cumulative amount received (not adjusted for inflation) would be $678,000 (using actuarial life expectancy). Clearly, the discounted present value of this expected receipt of income should be included in the calculation of net worth for financial planning purposes.

As you can see, $24 trillion in assets come from pension entitlements ($22.87 trillion) and life insurance reserves ($1.3 trillion), which represent 25% of total household net worth. According to the Fed, household financial assets were valued around $80 trillion. That figure includes cash, money market, and bank deposits at $11.25 trillion and bonds (US Treasury, agency, municipal, and corporate) at $3.9 trillion; the balance was comprised of US corporate equities, mutual fund shares, pension entitlements, and ownership in privately held companies.

Business ownership, which encompasses entities ranging from a New York hot dog stand to publicly listed corporations and privately owned multibillion dollar corporations, is the largest asset category on the balance sheet of American families (combined value of corporate equities, mutual fund shares, and equity in private businesses). For this reason, it is safe to say that American families are, directly or indirectly, business owners and that the profits derived from those businesses have been the most significant driver of wealth for the past 65 years.

Does the Federal Reserve's report give an unabridged perspective of US households' net worth? It does not. That's primarily because studying aggregated US household wealth does not provide insight into either the median family or those in the lower 50%. To gain further insight into the various subsets of US households, a study of MEDIAN (equal number above and below) as opposed to mean (average) net worth is in order. To illustrate how mean and median net worth differ, let's take a set of three families and assume one has a net worth of $1 million, one has a net worth of $100,000, and one has a negative net worth of $100,000 (e.g., a recent college graduate with accumulated student loan debt). Added together they total $1 million. Divide that number by 3 and you get a mean net worth of $333,000. While this number is mathematically correct, it inflates the second person's net worth by three and the third person's net worth by four while reducing the first's by two-thirds. A great distortion, I am sure you would agree.

Calculating median net worth can be equally distorting because it is based solely on the middle participant's net worth (whatever it may be). Using the above example, the median net worth of the group is $100,000. This reduces the wealthiest member's net worth by 90%, hits the middle person with 100% precision, and inflates the poorest by a factor of two.

Since our objective in studying this data is to gain perspective, I recommend studying both median and mean in order to broaden our understanding of the landscape. Unfortunately, however, the data on median wealth is sparse in comparison to mean wealth. The Federal Reserve report "Survey of Consumer Finances (SCF)," for example, only traces data back to 1989, whereas the mean household net worth report goes back to 1952.

Despite the drawbacks, by examining both mean and median, we can make some meaningful observations to gain a more informed view of the US household. For example, as of year end 2016, the SCF report states that between 2013 and 2016, the median net worth of families rose 16% to $97,300 (remember this number excludes future retirement benefits and life insurance) and mean net worth rose 26% to $692,100. The disparity is obvious, but what does it really signify? Studies such as the SCF report tend to simplify something that is inherently complex. When political posturing is added to the mix, the situation can become even more confusing.

As you read the following discussion, you'll see that studying the net worth of the Forbes 400 as a group creates similar distortions. But before we go on to our discussion of US households and the Forbes 400, I should note that while the Forbes 400 ranks members based on their total net worth, some analysts prefer to view the wealthiest Americans based on their adjusted gross income (AGI) as reported on their annual tax returns.

Using this method, for example, a tycoon business owner whom we will call Catherine, who sells her business for $100 million, will undoubtedly fall into the very top echelon of income tax filers for that year (the sale of a family business or stock position is considered income in the year of the liquidity event). That said, let's assume that Catherine pays her $20 million in long-term capital gains tax to the federal government and another $13 million in state and city taxes to New York State and New York City. Before any gifts to charity, the remaining $67 million might be expected to create an estimated 3% yield from dividends and bond interest (approximately $2 million annually).

While Catherine's taxable income in year two is still robust, her "income" (as measured by the AGI on her tax return) will have fallen by 98% from the year she sold the business to the subsequent year, and she will no longer rank among the wealthiest Americans based on her AGI. Of course, Catherine would still be considered wealthy even though her AGI fell by 98% and her total net worth fell by 33% (after the payment of capital gains taxes).

My point is that using the AGI as a measure rather than total assets as used to measure the Forbes 400 means that the spectacularly high "incomes" observed in the tax filings of Americans in any given year can include a once-in-a-lifetime event that is mathematically impossible to repeat in subsequent years. Thus, in the same way that median and mean paint very different pictures, so too does "total net worth" and "AGI." In talking about wealth it is important to look beyond the headlines to get an informed understanding of the changes in net worth over time.

Similarly, the top one-tenth of 1%, similar to the Forbes 400, and the Forbes 400 itself isn't necessarily composed of the same people every year. Some fall off entirely (in 2016, 26 fell off the list); some go up the list, some down. When looking at wealth it is important to look beyond the headlines to get an informed understanding of changes in wealth and net worth over time.

Dynamics Behind the Growth in Wealth

Throughout the rest of this chapter I will explore what factors drove the *mean* US household wealth compared to those that led an individual to be included in the Forbes 400. My goal in writing this chapter is not to debate the issues of wealth and income equality in American society. Rather, it is to inform you about some aspects of the topic that are seldom talked about and little understood. My aim is to study those things that drive wealth up as well as those that take it down.

If you are interested in seeing if you are getting more or less wealthy than your neighbor, a long-term study of US household net worth can be an effective yardstick. Similarly, I believe it is valid to compare the way the average American family's balance sheet has grown when compared with the growth in wealth of the Forbes 400. Forbes began compiling its list in 1982, so we'll take that as our starting point, but before we begin, it is important to note that the total wealth of the Forbes 400 families ($2.7 trillion as of October, 2017) represents only 2.8% of total US household wealth. The fact that the Forbes families own $2.7 trillion and the rest of us collectively own $94.3 trillion demonstrates that these comparisons are not only valid, but essential if we are to gain an informed view of American wealth.

In a parallel study of global billionaires, the Forbes 2018 Billionaires list included 2208 individuals from 72 countries (the Forbes 400 contains only Americans) with a combined net worth of $9.1 trillion,[2] which represents

---

[2] Forbes, "Meet The Members of the Three-Comma Club," March 8, 2018.

3.25% of the $280 trillion in global wealth (discussed above). That those on the global billionaires list own roughly the same percentage of global wealth as the Forbes 400 own as a percentage of American wealth might surprise some.

From 1982 to 2017 the average annual growth rate of the wealth of the Forbes 400 was 8.94% (the minimum rate of growth in net worth necessary to keep a person on the Forbes 400 list). Over that same period, the average annual growth rate of the average American household was 6.2%. When studying the reasons for this lower rate of growth in the wealth of the typical American household and the typical Forbes 400 family, one very obvious difference stands out: approximately 50% of American families' wealth is held in stocks and private businesses and the typical Forbes 400 family likely has 90% invested in these assets. Looking at Table 4.1, you will note that the ownership in private businesses (labeled Households and Nonprofit Organizations; proprietors' equity in non-corporate business) contains $11.6 trillion in assets. Assets listed as ownership in public company shares represent $17.8 trillion. Forbes doesn't give a definitive breakdown of the asset allocation of members of the 400 the way the Fed report does, but if you look at the percentage of stock ownership held by its more notable members including Messrs. Bezos, Buffett, and Gates, it is reasonable to assume a heavy concentration of business holdings.

Table 4.1 US household net worth

Components of US household net worth (year end 2017)	
Asset	Value in trillions $
Real estate and nonfinancial assets	34.00
Deposits, checking, and money market	11.39
Fixed income securities	3.91
Non-securitized loans	0.97
Corporate equities	17.88
Mutual fund shares	8.68
Receivables	0.30
Life insurance reserves	1.39
Pension entitlements	23.22
Equity in private businesses	11.61
Miscellaneous assets	1.06
Total assets	**114.39**
Liabilities (all debt, mortgages, consumer credit, and loans)	15.65
Net worth (Assets–liabilities)	**98.74**

It is also important to consider that in 1982, when the Dow Jones Industrial Average was still languishing at 1000—a 16-year plateau[3]—investors clearly didn't realize that 1982 would mark the end of the drought in stock prices (in 1966, the Dow Jones Industrial Average hit 1000 for the first time in history, a level that it would not break through until 1982). Between 1982 and 2017 the Dow went from 1000 to 25,000 and the price/earnings ratio went from 7 to 21. (We will discuss in great detail the way price-to-earnings [P/E] ratios and earnings yields drive the long-term performance of equity portfolios in Chap. 7.)

Another reason the average family performed at a slower pace than the business and stock-heavy Forbes 400 families is that in the 1980s the average family paid a huge amount in mortgage interest. According to freddiemac.com, the rate for a 30-year fixed rate mortgage in January 1982 was 17.48%. Granted, by the end of that year the rate had come down to 13.62%, but this mortgage interest still represented a massive amount of capital outflow for the typical family. Not only did those dollars spent on mortgage interest disappear from the family's balance sheet, it meant there were less dollars at work invested in businesses or stocks. Therefore, the 1982 to 2017 comparison can be mostly explained by these three variables: (1) the amount invested in private businesses; (2) the amount invested in stocks; and (3) the high mortgage interest rates.

There are interesting insights to be gained by comparing shorter periods of time within the available time periods. One notable example occurred between 1987 and 1990 when the average US household saw a faster growth in wealth than the Forbes 400 (6.96% for the mean US household versus 4.94% for the Forbes 400). This makes complete sense when you consider that the 1987 stock market crash (near the beginning of this period) and the stock market correction that followed Iraq's 1990 invasion of Kuwait (near the end of this period) had a greater impact on the Forbes families (heavily invested in stocks) than it did on the less heavily invested average US household. From 2000 to 2017, the Forbes 400s' wealth grew at a rate of 6.15% while the typical American family saw their net worth grow at a rate of 4.62%. Remember that the longer period, 1982 to 2017, experienced two 50% declines in stock prices (2000 dot-com bust and 2008 financial crisis), during which the business-heavy Forbes group undoubtedly took a larger hit. Remember also that the Forbes 400 represents the richest, and likely the most successful,

---

[3] I use the word "plateau" to describe the Dow performance from 1966 to 1982, even though during this 16-year period, large stock price corrections occurred; for example, in the late 1960s as well as in the "nifty fifty" crash of 1973–1975.

families of any particular period. Those who did NOT make the Forbes list in those years and were heavily invested in businesses may have fared much worse than those who did.

The spread between the average American family and the Forbes 400 tightens even more when you examine the period from 2008 to 2017. For this period, the Forbes 400 grew at a rate of 4.9% while the average American family grew at a rate of 3.85%. Again, the higher allocation to residential real estate (which fell during the financial crisis) affected the average family much more than it affected the Forbes families. While both stock and real estate prices would recover and surpass their 2008 peaks, the tighter correlation between the two groups exists because the downward and upward volatility affected both stock and real estate prices over this period.

Because the topic of income and wealth inequality has been such a widely discussed topic over the last decade, I expected to find a much wider variation between the Forbes 400 and the average family. The fact that the spread is only 2.74% per year over 35 years surprised me. One thing is certain: if the mean US household had reallocated its balance sheet to include a higher allocation to stocks and a lower allocation to real estate, the spread between them and the Forbes 400 would shrink if not completely disappear. Putting that into practical terms might be a choice most families would refuse to make: living in a smaller or cheaper home with the goal of having a larger retirement nest egg versus living more comfortably when they are younger and probably raising a family. You may know people—I do—who have 10% or less of their net worth in the value of their home in order to either retire early or robustly; you probably also know people whose largest asset is in the value of their home.

If it is true that a high real estate allocation was a significant contributor to the slower growth rate of the mean US household in comparison to the Forbes 400, then the converse is also true: if the Forbes 400 families reduced their ownership in stock and increased their ownership in residential real estate (in line with the 25% allocation of the mean US household), the spread between the two would shrink. It is important to understand that this choice (made very early in one's adult life) has a profound effect on the growth of wealth over decades, but I am in no way advocating that you limit the value of your home to 10% of your net worth! (I will discuss the drivers of stock prices in Chap. 7.)

*   *   *

My message to investors is to pay attention to the US household net worth numbers that come out of the Fed to keep informed about the character and footprint of American wealth. You can expect to see its findings in the headlines at least once per year.

The Forbes 400 list is a fascinating read because it represents a data set of real people who owned real businesses, and lived in our communities during our lifetime. Even making the Forbes 400 is a distant fantasy for most investors; reading about how a family grew their wealth and reached the very top allows us to connect to a "human story." It makes us realize that reaching that pinnacle may not be as fanciful as simply reading cold numbers makes it seem. Among the handful of members who managed to stay on the list since its 1982 debut, we can observe stark contrasts among three of them. Warren Buffett is a stock guy, with most of his net worth invested in the shares of the Berkshire Hathaway Corporation. Ross Perot, Sr. was reported by *Forbes* to have most of his wealth invested in municipal bonds,[4] and Donald Trump is widely believed to be heavily invested in real estate. If this is not an example of the way plummeting interest rates have affected stock, bond, and real estate prices over the last 35 years, I don't know what is.

Every October when the Forbes list is published, it makes a bit of a splash and headlines echo around the country and around the world about who is #1, who fell off the list, who's on it for the first time, along with all kinds of statistics about the industries that are the source of their wealth, their states of residence, and other assorted facts about its members. Despite all that's written and all the glossy photos of the top 25, there's a good deal of misunderstanding about it.

One of the greatest myths is that the list is static, that it represents the same people every year as if those who made it to the top of a mountain now spend their time kicking off those who are trying to join them. In 2012, Forbes reported that only 36 members of the original Forbes 400 1982 class were still on the list.[5] By 2017, the list of original members was down to 26. In other words, 374 of the original families were no longer on the list. Few readers even remember the name of the gentleman who was #1 on the Forbes list in 1982. Daniel Keith Ludwig, a builder of supertankers, topped the inaugural list with a net worth of $2 billion. Coincidentally, $2 billion was the minimum net worth needed to qualify for the Forbes list in 2017. Today a few bad hands of poker and a hefty dinner bill would cause Mr. Ludwig to drop off the list entirely, much less retain his spot at #1. Bill Gates, with a net worth $89

[4] Forbes.com, "The 17 Richest Living Veterans," May 26, 2011.
[5] Forbes, "The Forbes 400 Hall of Fame: 36 Members of Our Debut Issue Still In the Ranks," September 20, 2012.

billion, came in for the 24th consecutive year at #1 in 2017. A handful of recognizable names from the inaugural list still appeared in 2017, including Donald Trump, George Lucas, Nike founder Phil Knight, and Ross Perot, Sr.

In 1982, Jeff Bezos, whose 17% stake in Amazon allows him to boast a net worth of $109 billion (as of January 2018) and second place on the 2017 list, was only 18 years old when the original Forbes list was published. The list has been published for 35 years and with 400 spots on the list each year, theoretically there were 14,000 opportunities to appear on the list at least for one year. One statistic about the average annual growth in net worth necessary to stay on the list may surprise you: a member needed to achieve only 77% of the annual return of the S&P 500 index. There is a reason for this.

As I mentioned earlier in this chapter, 1982 marked the end of an era. That year, the Dow Jones Industrial Average traded at around 1000 and the S&P 500 traded around 100—the indices had hit 1000 and 100 for the first time in 1966, and oscillated above and below those levels until 1982. That's right, folks. The Dow and the S&P, which had been flat for 16 years, interrupted by short bull and bear cycles, began to move up. Reflecting the dismal performance of the markets and the heavy weight of double-digit inflation and high mortgage rates, the P/E ratio of the index was seven times. In 1982, there were no adherents to the "stocks for the long run" craze. Inverting the P/E to earnings yield (E/P) produced 14.29%. It should come as no surprise (and we will cover the effect of earnings yield on long-term stock performance in Chap. 7) that the annualized compound growth rate of the S&P 500 from 1982 to 2017 was 11.58%.

As I mentioned earlier, to stay on the Forbes list over the same period, the members' net worth had to grow at the rate of 8.94% AFTER taxes, AFTER day-to-day expenses for themselves and their families, and AFTER any fees paid to others to manage their fortunes.

This may come as unpleasant news for proponents of market index funds (such as the S&P 500 Index), because simply investing in the S&P wouldn't have netted 8.94% over the same timeframe. If investors were to earn 11.58% gross, they would lose approximately 2% to taxes (assuming a 6% state tax rate), 4% to spending, and let's assume 25 basis points for the investment management fee. After netting taxes, spending (normal withdrawals from the portfolio to cover living expenses and gifts), and fees, investors would be left with 5.33%.

For this same period, US household net worth grew at a rate of 6.2%, so investors in index funds would have failed miserably in their attempt to make or stay on the Forbes list (i.e., if they were relying solely on their portfolio for income without earned income from a job). They would also have failed to simply keep up with the average wealth of American families. While the above observation is not intended to wade into the active versus passive debate, it simply illustrates that an investor who held 100% of his wealth in an S&P 500 index fund and took annual income distributions would have underperformed the mean US household.

We will be making the Forbes data and the US household net worth calculator available to readers on our website www.wealthyinvestor.net so that you can examine specific time periods that interest you.

*   *   *

While my personal goals do not include making the Forbes 400, yours might, and, in my view, over time this is a benefit to all Americans. Let me explain, the composting of the wealth of the current Forbes 400 is already set to till back into the soil of the American economy. Consider this: If all of the Forbes 400 families ($2.7 trillion in 2017) spend 4% of their wealth per year ($100 billion), over the next two decades they will have spent $2 trillion. According to the Giving Pledge, 158 of the world's richest families have pledged to give $365 billion to charity over their lifetime or at death. Between spending and charitable pledges, 87% of the wealth of today's Forbes 400 families will leave their checkbooks and re-enter the economy.

In February of 2018, National Public Radio aired an interview with Microsoft founder, Bill Gates, on the news that he had dropped to the #2 spot on the Forbes Billionaires list, ceding the top spot to Amazon's Jeff Bezos. While Amazon's meteoric stock price rise was the primary driver of this ranking, there is another reason. Gates's wealth did not drop due to poor performance of Microsoft stock. It dropped because he decided to do something with it. On August 15, 2017, the *Guardian* reported that Gates had donated $4.6 billion to charity in that year, which reduced his ownership stake in Microsoft to just 1.3% of shares outstanding (in 1996, he owned 24%).

Just as college endowments benchmark their investment results versus their peers' through the annual National Association of College and University Business Officers survey, I believe the Fed's US Household Net Worth Survey is a valid broad benchmark against which individual investors can gauge whether they are "keeping up with the pack"—the average American family. Among wealthy families, the annual Forbes 400 minimum net worth is a widely available benchmark. On the other hand, there are many investors and wealthy families who say, "I don't care what other people do. I'm running my own race," a simple way of saying that the owner of wealth gets to call the tune and that it is one's attitude toward wealth—not an external, objective measure—that defines success or failure.

5

The Six Robbers of Wealth and How to Avoid Them

In *Investing Strategies for the High Net Worth Investor*, I stressed that the only dollars that were material to long-term success were those that stayed in the portfolio *net of* an investor's *spending, taxes, fees,* and *inflation.* To those wealth diminishers, two other things rob an investment portfolio of future success: *late starts* and *mistakes.* Many advisors and others who write about wealth accumulation focus on fees and then address the other five. In my view, this gets it completely backward. In this chapter, I approach each of these wealth robbers in their order of importance based on the magnitude of the dollar impact on the portfolios of investors who get these issues right versus those who don't.

Wealth Robber # 1: Late Starts

Few investment variables have as big a dollar impact on a portfolio than *when* the investor begins to invest and the *length of time* between that day and the day the portfolio is called upon to distribute capital. The investment blog getrichslowly.org highlights an excellent, but simple, illustration of the impact of timing on a portfolio. In their example, 20-year-old Britney decides to make a $5000 contribution to her Roth 401k. If the portfolio manages to achieve an 8% annualized return (the Roth enjoys a tax-exempt status), that $5000 investment will have grown to $180,000 by the time Britney is 65. Had she waited to make the investment until age 40, the same $5000 investment grows (at the same 8% return) to less than $40,000. By starting at age 20, the portfolio is worth four times what it would have been had she waited

© The Author(s) 2019

N. J. Gannon, *Tailored Wealth Management*,
https://doi.org/10.1007/978-3-319-99780-3_5

until age 40. Imagine the massive chasm that would exist between the two portfolios if Britney invested $5000 (at the same 8% return) every year.

Whatever the interest rate or the amount of money invested—whether our young investor earns 6%, or whether she invests $25,000 per year—time IN the investment is the biggest contributor to the outcomes available to her at age 65. Of course this is only a hypothetical situation. Financial calculators that simulate Britney's 45-year investment portfolio at 8% annualized exist only in theory. There is no investment that produces a constant, fixed rate of compounding. Even if an investor buys a 40-year maturity bond with a fixed, non-callable coupon rate, the re-investment rate of those bond coupons will fluctuate with the yields available in each year.

Wealth Robber # 2: Spending and Small Indulgences

Your daily cup of Starbucks, going out to lunch, your smartphone and satellite TV will cost you over $1 million over a lifetime. Think about that for a second and enter into a simple but dramatic exercise on Excel with me. Let's start with an 18-year-old who spends $5 per day on her artisanal cup of coffee. Instead of eating leftovers for lunch, let's give her a budget of $8 per day. Her monthly bill for her iPhone is $75 and she spends $45 per month on satellite TV, Spotify, or streaming movie services. These aren't things she has to have; they are simply nice to have. If you take those daily or monthly items and inflate them at 3% per year, our little spender has racked up over $600,000 cumulatively on those four indulgences by the time she is 65. If those habits continue for another 20 years, the cumulative cost rises to about $1.3 million by the time she has reached her 85th birthday.

I will concede that few of us go out to lunch every single day or that we will drink the 25,000 coffees included in our illustration. You will, as a young person, find other seemingly small indulgences in your life and agree that they indeed will add up over a lifetime. Of course, I am not suggesting that ALL readers switch to Folgers French roast, eat leftovers for lunch every day, skip the iPhone, and only watch free network TV. I use this illustration in order to shock you into realizing how much these habits cost over time and that it is simply your choice as to whether you will use your capital in that way. For those willing to drink the free coffee in the lobby, eat leftovers for lunch, skip the iPhone, and watch network TV, you have a $1 million head start versus the person to your right and left.

Wealth Robber # 3: Mistakes

Mistakes in the investment craft are a given. Warren Buffett makes them; Ronald Reade, our millionaire janitor, made them; I have made them, and you will certainly make them. The key is to minimize their number and size and to learn from your mistakes by which I mean to make a conscious effort NOT to fall into the trap of repeating an easily avoidable mistake.

A very common mistake investors make is to sell AFTER experiencing a precipitous decline in their portfolio. If an investor sells at the bottom, it can do irreversible harm, and for this reason it is critical for investors to understand WHAT they own and WHY they own it. I will talk later about active versus passive investing, but even if you have a financial advisor or wealth manager, there is no excuse for outsourcing or abdicating your responsibility for understanding the basics of your own investment portfolio. The above is a generalization; what follows are some real-life examples of what investor mistakes look like.

The panicked seller: In December 2008, a colleague recalled a regrettable story about one of his larger clients. This investor, whose portfolio at its peak (in 2007) was valued at around $15 million, became extremely nervous when, by December 2008, its value had declined to nearly $10 million. The portfolio was filled with high-quality blue-chip companies, such as Walmart common stock, that were not only profitable businesses, but ones that would grow their market share if the recession intensified. Nevertheless, the investor was nervous.

The advisor pleaded with the client to drive to his neighborhood Walmart and observe the activity in the parking lot. Was the parking lot full of customers walking out of the store after spending a couple of hundred dollars inside? Were there 18-wheeler trucks streaming in and out of the store's loading dock area? Was it likely that if the recession deepened even more (newly frugal minded) customers show up to shop there?

The client was unwilling to go through this exercise because, as his advisor told me, he didn't think of himself as an owner of the business. In his view the owners were the Walton family even though—based on the number of shares he owned—he received proportionally the same amount of the company profits they did. He thought of his position in Walmart as just another stock in his portfolio that looked like it was tanking.

When he told his advisor to liquidate just before Christmas, the advisor gave him this ultimatum. "As a registered advisor, I must comply with your direction to liquidate your portfolio, but I am unwilling to press the button.

If you decide to go forward, I will resign from your account and my colleague will execute your wishes. This is the wrong thing to do and I do not and will not take responsibility for creating a permanent loss in your account." The client understood and the portfolio was liquidated within the hour.

The client received a letter from his advisor the day after the liquidation confirming their conversation and recommending that the client refrain from ever investing in common stocks or funds. The advisor feared that once the market rebounded, the client would feel that he "missed out" and would take that $10 million and invest it into a peaking market only to repeat the process. The S&P 500 index closed the year at 865. The index bottomed 2½ months later, hitting an intra-day low of 666 on March 9, 2009. While the client had avoided another brief period of downside volatility, had he remained invested in the portfolio the value would have risen to over $30 million. As it happened, the man was happy to walk away with his check for $10 million.

My Advice: No investor should be invested in common stocks without recognizing and acknowledging the declines that earlier investors experienced. Here, I'm speaking principally about the great crash of 1929, the 16-year flat market from 1966 to 1982, the crash of 1987, the Japanese Nikkei crash of 1989, the dot-com burst of 2001–2002, and the financial crisis of 2008. I believe a conversation on this subject between the investor and her advisor is essential in order to either validate that she understands that crashes occur and is willing to accept that risk or trigger a more conservative asset allocation.

Regardless of whether investors acknowledge their risk appetite when they open an account, many develop amnesia and fear as the volatility they face appears to be a case of "this time it's different." I urge you to dig into Chap. 7 to develop an understanding of the earnings yield valuation method, which will give you a better and more informed view of the amount of risk and opportunity your portfolio carries. The unfortunate panicked investor I just described was likely counseled by his advisor and acknowledged his portfolio risk at the inception of the account, but, when faced with the loss, he simply changed his mind. Had he understood the earnings yield of the businesses (stocks) he owned, he would not have liquidated.

On May 19, 2010, I was interviewed along with others by CNBC about the incredible volatility of that day and that year. All of the other commentators explained why they believed the market was going lower. I acknowledged that on that day there was ash in the sky (the Icelandic volcano Eyjafjallajökull eruption that halted flights from Europe), oil in the water (the BP/Deepwater Horizon in the Gulf of Mexico was still gushing oil), and blood in the street (meaning Wall Street). But, I added, if investors simply looked at the net cash earnings of the businesses they owned, they would likely see an earnings yield of 8% or more and that simple arithmetic meant that bonds and cash were not better alternatives. The S&P 500 was at approximately 1080, which was a nice rally off the 666 intra-day level reached in March of 2009. Based on their remarks, I assume my fellow commentators were liquidating their own client portfolios. This was a day that posed a challenge for passive investors, hedge fund investors, and over-diversified investors either because their investment philosophy did not involve studying the underlying investments or because they simply held too many stocks in their portfolios to do this efficiently at such an emotionally charged time.

The Derivative Gambler: A few years after the release of *Investing Strategies* I received a call from the CEO of a local company who had read my book cover to cover. I was thrilled to take the meeting and eager to answer his questions. I was looking forward to his feedback. When we met, he had numerous Post-it notes on specific pages and had highlighted certain passages. At the end of an enjoyable meeting, he complimented the tone I took toward risk management in portfolios and then went on to share his father's experience.

His father was a finance professor at a prestigious European university. Beginning with a portfolio of about $2 million, his father developed a highly successful option trading strategy coming out of the trough of the dot-com bust in October of 2002. Option trading usually includes leverage (borrowed money/margin loans). The portfolio had such exponential success that by 2005, it was valued at over $50 million. By 2007, his portfolio topped $100 million. Along the way, word of the professor's success got out and a couple of college endowments asked him to invest a portion of their capital in his strategy.

As you might guess, to achieve those gains, he was heavily leveraged, and exposed to the financial and housing industries. The sunshine under which his portfolio basked likely faded when the opening salvos of the financial crisis were fired: the collapse of Bear Stearns and Lehman Brothers Holdings. Eventually his trades started to go against him, the margin loans were called, and position after position was force liquidated by his broker. He had placed bullish bets on a sector that was now in free fall and the fact that the accounts were leveraged derivatives sped the pace of the fall. From $100 million, his father was down to $10 million in equity. Still, he refused to exit. A temporary bounce gave him newfound confidence or hope, but soon the portfolio was down to $5 million. Although the portfolio was still double the value that he started with, he refused to hang up his cleats.

My Advice: Despite the "great recession," I still know doctors, business owners, lawyers, and others who dabble in the options market, day trade stocks or commodities, or participate in other high-risk investment behavior.

Some lessons are never learned. While there are a handful of skilled investors in the options market, their number pales in comparison to the numbers of ordinary investors who get hooked on the thrill of trading (whether it is options, day trading, or futures).

The professor's first mistake was that with $2 million in the bank he didn't think he was wealthy. He was more concerned with the next $2 million, then the next $5 million, then the next $25 million. At any point along the way, he could have stopped to take an inventory of what he had built and walked away. There is no crystal ball that will tell a speculator when it's time to get out. In all probability, the speculator educated himself about past collapses, but he is still surprised that what ignited *the collapse in which he finds himself has never before been observed, and thus could not have been predicted.*

The panicked investor, like our investor in Walmart and the professor, is not the only casualty of markets in freefall. I have witnessed billions of shares of stocks, mutual funds, and even bonds sold the day AFTER bad news comes out. For visual learners, pull up a long-term chart of NYSE trading volume and observe the spike that occurs at market bottoms. Remember also that for every seller on those huge volume days, there is a buyer on the other side of the trade. In recent years I saw the Mexican peso crisis of 1994, the Russian ruble crisis of 1998, the tech bubble of 2000, 9/11, the 2008 financial crisis, the 2011 Standard & Poor's downgrade of the US credit rating, Brexit, and so on.

Throughout each of these periods, markets were dislocated when leveraged investors could not meet margin calls and suffered forced liquidation. Next, hedge funds, index funds, and managed mutual funds receive redemption calls from their investors. A subsequent group of investors, wondering what the first two were thinking and whether another shoe is about to drop, decides to sell. Eventually, good businesses become priced so cheaply that patient capital comes in, provides pricing support, and ultimately prices rebound.

It is very important for investors to understand the magnitude of these stories just as it is to show the movie about railroad crossing collisions to new teenage drivers.

Over-Spenders: In the year 2000, *Stocks for the Long Run* was flying off the bookshelves. Companies were routinely offering early retirement packages to their employees and if you logged onto the popular investor websites, blogs, or financial periodicals an 8% portfolio return was called "conservative." It was not uncommon then for a union beer bottler, telephone lineman, or skilled worker to receive a lump-sum rollover of $1 million. Since investors often gravitate toward the advisor or company that tells them what they want to hear, many went into an all-stock portfolio mix chock full of tech, internet, or other hot stocks of the day. The advisor would "estimate" a 10% long-term return (which was mathematically impossible to achieve in 2000 when the earnings yield was 3% and the P/E ratio was 33), offer the investor a "conservative" 7% spending rate (planning to leave the other 3% in the portfolio for re-investment), and suggest rebalancing the portfolio periodically.

Do the math on what happened to the retiree (who was breathing a sigh of relief that Y2K didn't bring an end to the world) and started investing on January 2, 2000. The 7% spending rate meant $70,000 per year before taxes. Over the next three years, the investor would withdraw $210,000 (3 × $70,000), but, as it actually happened, between March 2000 and October 2002, the portfolio dropped by 50 to 60%. If a $1 million portfolio drops by 50% AND you withdraw $210,000, it is easy to see how the investor could get to zero (with some variation depending on the timing and size of the withdrawals).

My Advice: In Chap. 9, I will dig into the concept of setting realistic return assumptions. Over-spending and unrealistic return assumptions are avoidable mistakes. In 2000, we witnessed one of the rare periods where bonds were priced to outperform equities, yet investors routinely thumbed their noses at 6% tax-exempt municipal bonds and 7% US Treasuries in favor of overvalued equities.

Wealth Robber # 4: Taxes

One glaring error in the current presentations of some of the largest wealth management firms is that their investment recommendations are nearly identical no matter if the investments are in taxable or non-taxable accounts even though the research shows a loss of up to 50% on certain investments to taxes (high-turnover equity strategies, taxable bonds, and high-turnover hedge funds). How can it be that investors have not demanded a tailored wealth management platform that recognizes this very obvious issue?

To their credit, in recent years several mutual funds including Dodge & Cox, Vanguard, and others have begun weaving into their financial calculators AND their year end mutual fund annual reports an illustration of the reduced return experienced by investors holding their products in taxable accounts. Investors must still model for the effect of 0 to 13% state tax rates, but I applaud the increased disclosure in this area. Illustration of after-tax returns in the financial industry shouldn't be the exception practiced by a few. It should be the rule.

The next challenge is for those who advise investors at the portfolio level to factor the tax bite into long-term portfolio return assumptions.

My Advice: In *Investing Strategies* and subsequent updates to the models it contained, I illustrated that a taxable portfolio (taxed at the top bracket in a state like California) experienced a 35% loss of annualized investment return versus a non-taxable investment such as a 401k, pension, or endowment. I illustrated that the spread between stock and bond returns for taxable investments was much less than it was for non-taxable ones and I illustrated that there were several 20-year periods where bonds outperformed equities because of this diminished equity risk premium. Our study was the first, and, to this date, the ONLY one of its kind to examine the after-tax return of the S&P 500 inclusive of state taxation and liquidation costs at the top tax brackets. (For more on this study, see Chap. 11.) I will continue to update the study annually and publish the data from 1957 to the present at www.wealthyinvestor.net.

Readers of this book will be armed with the skills needed to perform this task themselves, but I call on investment advisors to respond to this very obvious data input in their long-term modeling for clients. Taxes can cost a portfolio 1.5 to 3% of long-term annualized returns (which may be 20 to 42% of the dollar return in any given year assuming a 7% long-term return). Investors should not settle for a pre-tax portfolio model from their advisors, but should demand to see net returns.

Wealth Robber #5: Inflation

My favorite example of the effects of inflation on retirees is one that involved two postage stamps which displayed a bobsled team. In 1972, one such stamp commemorating the Olympic Winter Games showed an artistic rendering of a bobsled team. The price of the stamp was 8 cents, the rate at the time for mailing a first-class letter. In 1994, 22 years later, a new bobsled stamp was released by the US Postal Service—its price, 24 cents. Observing the stamps, it's obvious the stamp commemorates the same sport, the tradition of the winter Olympic Games, and the fact that the cost of mailing a letter tripled.

The price of the stamp is an easy-to-understand example of the effect of inflation, and illustrates why investors must heed it, especially during the consumption phase of their portfolio when they will experience it to varying degrees. You might recall hearing about gold, real estate, or treasury inflation-protected securities as ways for investors to combat inflation. There is a better way: owning a business that has upward pricing power and benefiting from those inflated prices in the form of long-term profits and dividends. Coke, McDonalds, Colgate, and Procter & Gamble are examples of companies that routinely exercise their pricing muscle in the marketplace.

In the context of a diversified portfolio, it should be acknowledged that bonds cannot combat future price inflation since the rate of return earned by the investor at the time of purchase is fixed. However, there have been a few occasions where bonds did an effective job fighting inflation. The most notable example was 1982, when treasury bonds yielding 14% compensated investors for a future inflation that never materialized. Those who missed out on buying bonds in the early 1980s missed the biggest free lunch in a century!

My Advice: Recognize that inflation will play a role in your future spending. You'll be able to mitigate some of the effects by refusing to pay inflated prices for things you don't really need. It is also important to understand that you need not assume a constantly growing rate of annual consumption in the later years of your retirement when you no longer wish or are no longer able to do all the things you did at 20 or 40 or even 60.

Wealth Robber # 6: Fees

While fees don't have the same magnitude of impact that taxes, mistakes, or over-spending have, they do have a notable effect on portfolio returns. I submit to those who focus solely on fees (while remaining silent on taxes, spending, and mistakes) that adopting a 100% passive portfolio has not proved to be a panacea for investment portfolios as measured by annual surveys.

Fees on investment portfolios vary widely. The largest institutional portfolios, such as the $320 billion CalPERS, pay approximately 35 basis points (0.35%) across all of their investments. Many balanced mutual funds such as the Vanguard Wellington and the Dodge & Cox Balanced have internal fees ranging from 0.35 to 0.5%. Many retail investment clients pay an advisory fee of 1% on assets; however, this fee encompasses portfolio management as well as personal financial planning, estate planning, and cash flow management.

My Advice: It is important for investors to strike the right balance on the fee equation and for them to understand the pros and cons of each of the decision points that lead them to their preferred method. It is a mistake, in my opinion, to begin the investment discussion with fees and *only then* delve into the other facets of portfolio management. It simply makes no mathematical sense to let the variable that may have the smallest impact on long-term returns have the heaviest weighting on the decision-making process. Instead, the investor must get the items that have the biggest impact correct first, and THEN go about optimizing their particular situation for fees. Certainly, an investor would be better off in a fund that had a 1% fee and a 9% annual return than a fund that had a 0.15% fee and a 7% annual return.

Sources of Information: To give you an idea of fees, we'll now look at several sources: Campden Global Family Office Report, National Association of College and University Business Officers, various endowments.

The Global Family Office Report 2017, produced by Campden Research, offers a granular view of the fees paid by family office portfolios. The report contains data from the survey of 262 global family offices with average assets under management of $921 million. On average, total costs (inclusive of operating expenses, outside manager investment fees, and outside manager performance fees) were 1.2%. Investment managers' fees averaged 24.7 basis points, performance fees averaged 22.7 basis points, and internal administrative costs organic to the family office and its staff were 73.3 basis points. Does your advisor produce an annual report that shows what you kept net of all fees and taxes? If you pay taxes at the top brackets, demand that your advisor produce this number *or* educate yourself on how to calculate it. Don't just ignore it.

Investor Beware

I dedicated a whole chapter to these wealth robbers because formulating a long-term investment process assumes that you'll sidestep or minimize the impact of them. You may already have committed a few of them; if so, you'll need to protect yourself from future mistakes in order to maximize your returns. That means you have to start today. If you are young and just starting out, you probably haven't made these mistakes, so read this chapter again and resolve not to make them. They will rob you of wealth.

6

The Wealth Lifecycle: From Building It to Passing It On

Driving a car, flying a plane, scuba diving, and sky diving are examples of somewhat complex activities that require instruction, study, examination, and practice. The process of becoming or STAYING wealthy doesn't come with an instruction or maintenance manual. While other authors have covered this topic, I believe it is fit to meet readers where they are in life and render what I believe to be sensible habits and perspectives so that their journey forward can be more effective.

If you were to review bestselling titles about personal wealth management on Amazon, you would find that many are filled with advice on how to dig yourself out of a hole. I believe we adequately covered the subject of wealth robbers in the previous chapter, so in this chapter I'd like to address the various constituencies, who, I hope, are readers of this book. In doing so, I am assuming that each has an open mind *and* the willingness to adopt certain behaviors I will recommend.

With that in mind, it makes the most sense to start at the beginning—with young people, as the habits of saving, frugality, and work ethic see their biggest development in the first two decades of life. Many autobiographies of wealthy people include stories that begin something like this: "I'll never forget the first dollar I earned mowing lawns in the neighborhood" or "My grandmother told me that if I watch the pennies, the nickels and dimes will take care of themselves." Maybe you can't recall a particularly succinct lesson about wealth or saving from your youth. Most people don't. Not to worry. We'll fill in the blanks as we move along.

© The Author(s) 2019
N. J. Gannon, *Tailored Wealth Management*,
https://doi.org/10.1007/978-3-319-99780-3_6

Stage 1: Youth

If you are reading this and haven't finished high school, you must. $35,000 to $50,000 per year jobs are waiting for those who complete a technical college like Ranken Tech in St. Louis or a similar institution in your hometown. The president of Ranken Tech, Stan Shoun, who spends much of his time drumming up financial support for scholarships, admits that the lack of a GED is a huge barrier to entry for young people who want to better themselves. If you are one of the many community volunteers who work to help youngsters pass their GED exam, bless you. You are changing lives when you help someone get over this hurdle, and, if you happen to encourage them continue their education by getting an associate's or bachelor's degree, which can lead to a well-paying job, you can take partial credit for bringing them into the top 5% of global wage earners.

To the mothers and fathers reading this book: Don't let your children drop out of school. We must ensure that our young people finish high school, and for those who haven't, we must make GED programs as practical and available as they can be.

To the teenagers reading this book: I strongly recommend that as soon as you turn 16 you pursue and land a job on weekends during the school year and summer breaks that will allow you to begin making money. There is nothing available to you in high school or in college that will hone your wealth-building skills better than earning a paycheck.

To those reading this book who choose not to go to college: Whether your decision is for either personal or financial reasons, it is important to solicit input from people in your life who seem to be constantly bettering themselves. The name of one of my favorite meat cutters at my local market is Steven. He is great at his job, great with customers, and always smiling. The job pays about $35,000 per year and includes full health insurance.

Steven works the afternoon shift and, in the morning, attends our local community college. He is pursuing an associate's degree with an eye toward becoming a licensed occupational health therapy assistant (OTA). There are unfilled jobs for those with this qualification, so his outlook is bright. When he flips the switch from meat cutter to OTA, his salary will jump 60% to $56,000 per year. He is a great guy and I love hearing how he has navigated his career with an eye toward continual improvement. I doubt Steven allows himself to be surrounded by negative people. My hope is that the positive outlook on life that Steven embodies rubs off on people around him: family, friends, and even co-workers.

In my view, if a young person has a passion for a particular middle-class career such as firefighting, elementary school teaching, or military service they shouldn't let anyone steer them away from it simply to chase more dollars. People in all walks of life who adopt sensible financial habits can live a happy and rewarding existence. I am impressed with the way Steven made this decision.

Stage 2: Young Adult

If you are to become wealthy, you will first need to conscientiously adopt and practice delaying gratification. To begin, on day 1 of your first job, you need to save the maximum allowable contribution to your 401k or retirement plan; usually that's 15%. I am literally astounded at the number of young people who refuse to max their 401k contribution, including those who willingly throw away the employee matching dollars that are available to them. Don't sign an apartment lease or a car loan until you have signed up for the maximum. Your chances of becoming wealthy in the future hinge heavily on this decision.

I take my hat off to my older brother, Sean, who convinced me that I could afford to contribute $1980 per year from my starting salary of $13,200. Thank you, Mom and Dad, for allowing me to live at home that first year so I could begin the savings habit on the right foot. New college graduates have many opportunities to climb the ladder from that first day on the job and, since, I hope, you will be no stranger to thinking big, commit yourself to growing into saving 25 to 50% of your gross earnings *as your salary grows*. Don't be like Clarke Griswold from the classic *National Lampoon's Christmas Vacation* film waiting for the year-end bonus to hit so you can put in a swimming pool. That is no way to live. If you are successful, you should allow your salary to grow faster than your lifestyle. Doing this will give you massive choices when you are 40 or older. *Commit to a large savings rate from the start.*

As you develop your investment and savings skills, you must focus on where you hope to go in your life. If you see yourself spending evenings at the country club and summers at the shore, you better commit yourself to out-working the women and men in the cubicles next to yours. While this is no guarantee of success, it is also true that those who work till 7 or 8 p.m. are often rewarded for their effort. Each of you has the right to run your own race and to play your own game, just don't resent co-workers when they sacrifice sleep, family, and free time in order to shine in front of their customer, and that includes their boss.

Some of my colleagues routinely play a game of "what if" on this very subject. "What if the firm offered you $10 million a year, but you had to move to New York and work 90-hour work weeks? Would you do it?" Most answer no. As I said, it all depends on what you want in life, and there is no right or wrong answer as long as you invest and save to meet those goals.

Stage 3: The Middle Years

There are many employees in businesses large and small who love their jobs and wouldn't want to be the department manager, much less the CEO. These folks smile throughout the workday; they enjoy what they do and the way they interact with others. They wouldn't want their boss's job for any salary. These folks are very often wealthy in mind and habit. I remember one woman who worked in the same company as I did. I believe she had the same position for 15 years making a wage of around $75,000 per year. She owns her home and has no mortgage. She is proud of that home. She is happy with the choice she made.

One day, I asked her how she enjoyed her Easter holiday. "It was wonderful," she said. "I took my nephew to Paris. Neither of us had ever been, so I decided to take him." How great is that? I imagined her watching the twinkling lights on the Eiffel Tower on a cool April evening sipping a sassy little glass of Bordeaux. I'm certain she didn't stay in a five-star hotel near the Champs-Élysées, but I am sure she enjoyed it better than many who do. I admire how she struck a balance in her life.

Stage 4: Late Middle Age

You have big plans and dreams. You work hard and deserve success. It's time now to reread my advice to the young adult just climbing the career ladder. If your country club dues, mansion mortgage, and Audi S-7 payment require the bulk of your paycheck, you are less likely to and may never become wealthy. If this book has caught you mid-career, there is still time. Don't spend a dime of your next raise and if you think you are over-stretched, downsize. You will be proud to tell that story to your children when they have children of their own, and you will have served as a great example. You will make many sacrifices along the way, so consider the trade-offs, such as missing your children's childhood, and consider how you would feel in the event that you do

NOT become the CEO—not everyone gets there—and find yourself among the many casualties of corporate achievers.

If you have successfully mastered the art of climbing the corporate ladder, you may be tempted to lessen or eliminate practicing the art of delayed gratification or to weaken your financial plan for savings. The fancy watch, the new sports sedan with the theater sound system, the new house in the desirable up-and-coming neighborhood will begin to tempt you. Whether or not you allow yourself to give in to one or more of these temptations is, of course, a personal decision that should be made by you and your family.

What you (and they) should not do is buy into a lifestyle, betting on your next raise or bonus. When you begin dreaming on Zillow about the new house with the swimming pool and fire pit you'll know in your gut whether or not you can afford it. Before jumping in, consider other factors that can affect your financial situation. Perhaps, for example, your spouse wants to stay home with the children or return to school full time or you've decided you want take time off and travel the world. These might be perfectly doable if you stay where you are, but could create a financial strain if you move up.

Stage 5: Final Decade before Retirement

Whether you are the CEO of your company or find yourself somewhere else on the corporate ladder, it is important to make preparations to "land the plane." I suggest that members of this group reread Chap. 3 and ask themselves this important question, "how much is enough?" In my 27 years managing portfolios and advising investors, I continue to be amazed at the number of senior executives with eight- or nine-figure portfolios who refuse to reduce the risk and concentration in their portfolios.

Earlier in the book, we discussed the lack of control even the management team of a company has on the P/E multiple its stock commands. We also discussed the unknowns relating to the character and timing of the next recession or bear market. Much as we don't want to think about it, most of us know that we don't know how many more years we have to live. For all these reasons, it is imperative that you use this decade to prepare for retirement.

Economic factors aren't the only variables that should be weighed as to when one should retire. Do you or your spouse, if you are married, have a history of heart disease in your family? What about Alzheimer's disease occurring before the age of 70? If you haven't purchased long-term care insurance, this is the time to consider doing so. Alternatively, you may choose to self-insure. Before making that decision, have a conversation with your family attorney and your financial advisor about how best to plan for this possibility.

This is also the time to think about the future. My friend Tony Gallea put it to me this way, "When the bar chart of your net worth is still rising, and the number of years you have remaining to live is diminishing, you must determine whether the lines have crossed." Thus, he decided that when there is an abundance of financial resources and a shortage of potential years, it is futile to solely focus on your net worth while putting off the days that you could spend enjoying a more relaxing life doing the things you hoped to accomplish in retirement. I know many people who worked hard at their careers happily until the age of 75 or beyond. If you love it, have at it. If you are only doing it for the money, this question deserves more deliberation.

Stage 5: Parenthood

While parenthood can come at almost any time in the lifecycle, whenever it does occur, for most people, it feels like another stage and a time to think about (rethink) goals and lifestyle. Most would agree that negative personal traits can be learned and reinforced in the home, that is, children imitating what they see their parents and others do. Racism, wastefulness, laziness, and verbal abuse are learned traits. Positive traits such as open-mindedness, resourcefulness, sharing, and frugality are also learned traits.

Every August, approximately five million new college freshmen migrate from their homes to the welcome team at their freshman dormitory. A large number of them place a premium coffee maker such as a Keurig or Nespresso machine on the luggage trolley to go into their room. A good number of them will then do what Starbucks's business plan loves: they will buy a $4 to $5 Starbucks coffee every day. According to a 2015 article in *The Atlantic*, a daily cup of brewed coffee comes to $307 per year; a pod-cup costs $723; and a $4 daily Starbucks costs $1467 per year. Multiply each of these drinks by four years of college and it costs brewed coffee drinkers $1228; $2892 for pod-cup drinkers, and $5840 for the Starbucks drinkers. The difference in cost between Starbucks and brewed coffee comes to $4612 over a four-year college career.

What role do parents play in their child's decision to choose one or the other? Parents have a choice to make regarding their child's needs versus their wants. Many of the parents who naively purchased the coffeemaker during the college dorm shopping trip also end up "padding" their kid's accounts after their son or daughter depleted them on pumpkin-spiced lattes. Parents who are unwilling to let their college student tough it out with a cup of Folgers French Roast because he or she burned through their spending money will be weakening their ability to make more important financial decisions as they move forward in life. I am not picking on Starbucks or college kids here; I am simply stating that the habit of replenishing your child's spending account when you know it was spent on "wants" versus "needs" is something that can have a deleterious effect over time.

In my view, such things as a summer job to pay for a college student's incidental expenses during the year are a necessity. Working one or two days a week at a campus job to earn additional spending money is a valuable life lesson. Parents who wish to provide their kids with a little extra during the year might consider a summer salary match based on the wages they earned over the summer at the local pizza place or store at the mall. In doing this, you have created a cause and effect; you have demonstrated that the second dollar is possible only if the first dollar is earned. Be brave enough to say "no" to the bank account refresh. Your child will be able to sustain life on their meal plan in the cafeteria.

Stage Six: Twilight Years

Perhaps you are now a wealth creator; if so, it's time to prepare for your "heirs and affairs." You have created something, likely, beyond your own wildest dreams. There were no handbooks that led you to where you stand today. Similarly, deciding to do what is best for those who come after you can be a daunting task. Elsewhere we will discuss philanthropy and deciding how or if to go big, by, for example, making the Giving Pledge or doing something similar.

"I cannot control my heirs from the grave," said one of my good friends. This is a wise statement, and it may be one of the many reasons people make the Giving Pledge or leave all their estate to charity. Some are altruistic; others not. Imagine, for example, leaving $100 million to a child or grandchild who despises the sound of your name. It happens all the time. Don't let it. I can say with confidence that it is better to leave your fortune to the American Red Cross, Catholic Relief Services, or some other organization devoted to the greater good than to someone simply by virtue of being related. Likewise, if you think your descendants will sue one another, become jealous of one another, adopt a life of leisure or entitlement, composting your wealth back into the ecosystem may be the best thing. Everybody hates a bitter rich guy. Don't be responsible for creating one more.

Fortunately, what I just described is a worst-case scenario. There are so many examples of heirs doing great things in the world, bettering the family name, and exponentially seeding the ground with gratefulness and a sense of duty. Some go into the army, become members of helping professions—teachers, doctors, social workers, and so on are great parents and community members.

Later, I advise heirs to live a life of gratitude; here I say, be grateful. You worked very hard for what you have, and now you must decide what you would like to happen with it when you are gone.

I have seen families create so many trusts and entities that, by the time the wealth creator has passed, nobody understands either them or the reason they were created in the first place. It doesn't make you a bad person to simply pay your estate taxes and split what is left among your kids, free and clear. If you make it to 85, they may get it at 65, at which time they can enjoy *their* golden years. Had you not become so wealthy, this is likely what would happen as it does to most families. If you opt for the simple as opposed to the complex, there is merit in doing that even if, by not pulling every estate planning lever, your family is left with a few dollars less after paying estate taxes.

Your objective, in your twilight years, is to behave in a way that shows your love for your family, hoping that love will last after you have passed. You have the opportunity to nail the perfect pitch. You get to decide which one warrants a swing; just don't wait too long.

To heirs of wealthy families: Some call you a member of the "born on third base" club or "trust fund babies." Yet you never asked, or were given a voice in, whether you wanted to join the club, but here you are. Some of the things that now affect your life were put into place before you were born or when you were very young. Those making decisions tried their best to draft a plan with the data they had available to them at the time. Rarely are these plans perfect. One day, you may be called into an attorney or wealth manager's office and be given some very good news: you have been given a gift. You didn't earn it; you didn't do anything to deserve it; you simply must accept that someone else has given you a gift. In most cases, this relative was a parent, grandparent, or aunt or uncle. While they didn't know what your life would entail today, they made the gift in good faith hoping that it would bring good things.

Too often, members of your "club" react to inherited wealth the way Superman reacts to Kryptonite. It weakens them or robs them of the opportunity to build and live an ordinary life. Some of you may never have the thrill someone of less wealth feels on the day they pay their last mortgage installment and burn it in their fire pit because your first home was purchased for you. Most of you have read or heard about the spectacular loss and disappearance of wealth after a person wins the lottery. Many regret the day they turned in the ticket. This doesn't have to be you. The most salient advice I can give you is to meditate on gratefulness, one of the most powerful feelings a human can have. You have a destiny in life and that shouldn't change because you have a trust fund. A trust fund should be viewed as the cherry on top of the cake, not as a burden.

Regardless of whether you inherited the family name, you have the right, if not the obligation, to become the first of YOUR generation to do something special. You can begin thinking about how your actions today might bring great things to your children, to grandchildren, or to society as a whole. If your cup runneth over, shouldn't YOU think about creating your own family foundation OR making contributions to your family's namesake foundation? While you owe respect and gratitude to the relative who gave you the gift, it was only money. To the extent that you have been given a choice, every path remains available to you. Whether you become a schoolteacher, a social worker, a music composer, or even a corporate CEO, use the gift to help get you where you are going. Never let that gift lead you or define you. Wealth, career success, philanthropy can be as much a part of your life as anybody else's. Don't let the fact that you have a trust fund to keep you from feeling the wind of personal success on your back.

If someone talks about you behind your back, calling you a "trust fund baby," your best bet is to prove them wrong by becoming successful, achieving the destiny you have envisioned for yourself. Being an heir to wealth (or talent) can give you a tremendous opportunity to live a comfortable life and pursue a meaningful career of your own. You may be given the opportunity to steward the funds in your family foundation. What an honor that is—one that pays tribute to the person who gave you your gift. If you decide to make the family foundation your life's work, get your hands dirty. Go to Haiti and meet the people you are helping. Have lunch in the cafeteria of the inner city school where you made a grant to purchase musical instruments for the students. Put yourself in the buffet line to give a hamburger to the workers who are filling sandbags holding back the flood. You can be great at anything. Breathe in the gratitude of what was given to you; then own and be proud of what you did with it.

Part II

Technical Aspects of Tailored Wealth Management

7

The Efficient Valuation Hypothesis: The Long View

Tailored Wealth Management is a fitting title for this book because wealthy investors experience markedly different outcomes in managing their wealth, which makes a "one size fits all" approach ineffective. When I wrote *After-Tax Returns on Stocks* Versus *Bonds for the High Tax Bracket Investor*[1] in 2006, it was the first to study the topic, including the impact of state taxation, from the inception of the S&P 500 Index to the present day. That paper launched my passion for doing independent financial research, led to my first book deal with McGraw-Hill, and has continued to inspire me to explore related topics. The results of that study have withstood over a decade without refutation or an alternate thesis. When we conducted it, we created rolling 20-year periods not only to study the net impact on portfolios, but also to look at the specific economic data that was available to investors at the beginning of each of those periods.

Cause and effect is a theme that runs throughout this book, and I am more than ever convinced that it is time to challenge two theories: (1) that stock prices are random and (2) that prices revert to their mean, two widely held theories used by wealth management firms, academics, and robo-advisors.

In this chapter, I present an updated version of that paper, co-authored with Scott Seibert, CFA, and re-titled "Forecasting Long-Term Portfolio Returns: The Efficient Valuation Hypothesis."[2] I have two hopes for the

---

[1] *The Journal of Wealth Management*, Fall 2006, http://www.efalken.com/pdfs/BlumGannonaftertaxreturns.pdf. I am grateful to Charlotte Beyer, who insisted that I study the topic, and to Jean Brunel, editor of *The Journal of Wealth Management*, for allowing me to share the results of my research.

[2] *Seeking Alpha*, March 6, 2018, www.seekingalpha.com. Scott Seibert, CFA, my co-author, has been a faithful companion on this work. You can read more of his work in *The Journal of Wealth Management*.

© The Author(s) 2019
N. J. Gannon, *Tailored Wealth Management*,
https://doi.org/10.1007/978-3-319-99780-3_7

research and the lessons I am attempting to convey: first, that after a decade in, the work withstands the scrutiny and debate that it is sure to engender among adherents of competing hypotheses. Second, that if we missed something or failed to include some variable, we hope the paper ignites debate and becomes the impetus for an even better, more reliable theory to replace the Efficient Valuation Hypothesis. I will be happy with that. For now, I hope you read and study this hypothesis and consider, after reviewing the data from 1957 to 2017, whether you can still conclude that over the long run stock prices are random.

Study the data and examine the subsequent performance of portfolios based upon the earnings yield at the beginning of each period and decide for yourself whether stock prices "cling" to a statistical mean OR whether studies of "mean reversion" (the theory that assumes prices and returns eventually revert toward their average) have resulted in failure since the year 2000 (and other periods). See whether you can say that it was impossible to predict the "lost decade" beginning in 2000 or, instead, that it was predictable, but something investors completely missed. Ask yourself whether indexing the S&P 500 produced a satisfactory risk-adjusted return for investors when the 20-year performance markedly under-performed the long-term average. Challenge me and Scott Seibert; tell us if we have missed something or gotten this completely wrong.

Forecasting Long-Term Portfolio Returns: The Efficient Valuation Hypothesis

Forecasting long-term asset class returns with reliability is an important component for matching a portfolio's performance with its future liabilities. Whether one is an individual investor or a public pension fund, a reliable estimate of an asset's minimum expected return is critical for financial planning purposes. Using the US public pension system as an example, the use of inflated return expectations has perpetuated a growing deficit. According to Moody's, in 2017, US public pension plans had unfunded liabilities of over $4 trillion. A deficit this massive can be rectified only by either cutting previously promised benefits for current participants or having future generations pick up the difference through higher contributions, sacrificing their standard of living. Most investors have an understanding that inception yield is predictive of the future returns of a fixed income (bond) portfolio. We aim to illustrate that starting earnings yields are similarly predictive of the future returns in an equity portfolio, over 20-year investment periods.

Much of the previous financial research suggests either forecasting future returns is a futile exercise because returns are random, or that asset class performance tends to display a reversion to the mean of its historical observations. Eugene Fama, known for developing the Efficient Market Hypothesis, famously stated:

> Most simply the theory of random walks implies that a series of stock price changes has no memory-the past history of the series cannot be used to predict the future in any meaningful way. The future path of the price level of a security is no more predictable than the path of a series of cumulated random numbers. (*Random Walks in Stock-Market Prices* 1965)

Among those who adhere to the theory of mean reversion, Jeremy Siegel wrote in *Stocks for the Long Run* (2007) that stock returns "cling" to a statistical trend line. In reality, for the first 18 years of the twenty-first century, the total return on the S&P 500 index (with dividends re-invested) was only 5.34%, approximately 50% lower than its often-quoted long-term average of 10%. Was this dramatic under-performance of stocks for such an extended period truly a function of randomness? Does the degree of this under-performance weaken the theory of reversion to the mean? Our analysis seeks to narrow the gap between an investor's equity return *expectations* and the actual future returns received. We aim to illustrate, utilizing 20-year rolling periods, that equity returns and portfolio performance over the long run do not perform randomly, but rather are remarkably predictable.

Hypothesis

The study seeks to demonstrate that much of the long-term (20-year rolling periods) variability in stocks can be explained by the beginning-of-period earnings yield (the inverse of the starting P/E ratio). If our hypothesis is correct, investors can plan for future using a forecasted minimum expected return to be realized over a 20-year investment horizon.

Method Description

A typical 20-year investment horizon includes multiple business cycles, possibly comprised of unexpected economic events, which have the potential to add or subtract from investment returns over the analysis period. According to the National Bureau of Economic Research the United States has experienced 11 business cycles during the modern era, 1945–2009. The average cycle length, whether measured from trough from previous trough or peak from previous peak, is roughly 69 months, or 5.75 years. We seek to neutralize the impact of outsized returns derived from a single business cycle by focusing on 20-year rolling periods. In choosing the beginning-of-period P/E ratio as the starting point for our analysis, we have selected a measure of valuation that is widely available and well understood by investors.

Time Period

A total of 42 rolling full calendar year 20-year periods exist in the analysis period, which begins at the inception date of the S&P 500 on January 1, 1957, and ends December 31, 2017 (1957–2017). Each rolling 20-year period has its own annualized return.

Annualized Returns

The 20-year annualized rolling returns from the S&P 500 are presented. The returns are displayed as a pre-tax and pre-liquidation return of the S&P 500, over each 20-year period.

P/E

The price-to-earnings ratio is presented as of January 1 of the beginning year of each 20-year period.

Earnings Yield

The earnings yield of the index is derived from taking the inverse of the P/E ratio at the beginning of each period (January 1).

Return: EY

The beginning-of-period earnings yield is compared to the actual 20-year annualized return produced during the 20-year period. The difference between the actual annualized return and the earnings yield is displayed.

Exhibit 1 Correlation of 20-year annualized return pre-tax

Correlation of 20-year annualized return pre-tax, pre-liquidation vs. beginning-of-period (Jan 1) earnings yield			0.83
Time period	20-year annualized return	Beginning of period (Jan 1)	20-year annualized return-EY
Beg (Jan)–end (Dec)	Pre-tax, pre-liquidation	P/E	Earnings yield
1957–1976	7.81%	13.3×	7.52%	0.29%
1958–1977	7.79%	11.9×	8.40%	−0.62%
1959–1978	6.42%	19.1×	5.24%	1.18%
1960–1979	6.99%	17.7×	5.65%	1.34%
1961–1980	8.26%	18.7×	5.35%	2.92%
1962–1981	6.76%	21.2×	4.72%	2.04%
1963–1982	8.23%	17.2×	5.81%	2.42%
1964–1983	8.22%	18.2×	5.49%	2.72%
1965–1984	7.72%	17.8×	5.62%	2.11%
1966–1985	8.55%	17.4×	5.75%	2.80%
1967–1986	10.03%	14.9×	6.71%	3.32%
1968–1987	9.18%	17.7×	5.65%	3.53%
1969–1988	9.45%	18.2×	5.49%	3.96%
1970–1989	11.41%	15.1×	6.62%	4.79%
1971–1990	11.05%	16.7×	5.99%	5.06%
1972–1991	11.78%	18.3×	5.46%	6.31%
1973–1992	11.23%	19.1×	5.24%	5.99%
1974–1993	12.60%	12.3×	8.13%	4.47%
1975–1994	14.33%	7.3×	13.70%	0.63%
1976–1995	14.35%	11.7×	8.55%	5.80%
1977–1996	14.30%	11.0×	9.09%	5.21%
1978–1997	16.35%	8.8×	11.36%	4.98%
1979–1998	17.43%	8.3×	12.05%	5.38%
1980–1999	17.56%	7.4×	13.51%	4.04%
1981–2000	15.42%	9.1×	10.99%	4.43%
1982–2001	14.96%	8.1×	12.35%	2.62%
1983–2002	12.52%	10.2×	9.80%	2.72%
1984–2003	12.80%	12.4×	8.06%	4.74%
1985–2004	13.04%	9.9×	10.10%	2.94%
1986–2005	11.79%	13.5×	7.41%	4.38%
1987–2006	11.66%	16.8×	5.95%	5.71%
1988–2007	11.64%	15.4×	6.49%	5.15%
1989–2008	8.34%	11.5×	8.70%	−0.35%
1990–2009	8.12%	14.5×	6.90%	1.22%
1991–2010	9.03%	14.6×	6.85%	2.18%
1992–2011	7.72%	21.6×	4.63%	3.09%
1993–2012	8.12%	20.9×	4.78%	3.34%
1994–2013	9.11%	17.3×	5.78%	3.33%
1995–2014	9.72%	14.5×	6.91%	2.81%
1996–2015	8.02%	16.3×	6.12%	1.90%
1997–2016	7.59%	18.2×	5.49%	2.10%
1998–2017	7.11%	22.0×	4.54%	2.57%

Results

Using the earnings yield as a minimum expected return, the hypothesis was successful at a rate of 95%. Over the 42 periods, only two scenarios had a realized annualized return less than the beginning-of-year earnings yield "forecast." The two periods that didn't meet the minimum expected return were 1958–1977 and 1989–2008. For 1958–1977, an annualized return of 7.79% was realized versus an earnings yield forecast of 8.40%, which resulted in a missed forecast of −0.62%. In 1989–2008, an annualized return of 8.34% was realized versus an earnings yield forecast of 8.70%, which resulted in a missed forecast of −0.35%. A couple of similarities exist with the two periods that didn't meet the forecasted earnings yield. First, both of the earnings yields fell in the 75th percentile of all starting earnings yields. Also, in both scenarios the last year of the analysis period was a negative total return year for the S&P 500. In 1977 the total return was −6.76% and −36.12% in 2008. The combination of a high earnings yield forecast plus a negative return in the final year of the analysis partially contributed to the missed forecasts.

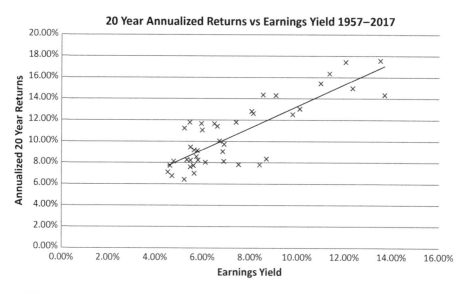

Exhibit 2   20-year annualized returns 1957–2017

In Exhibit 2, we have plotted the annualized 20-year returns versus earnings yield from the 42 periods that were observed in the analysis. The correlation of the data sets as shown in Exhibit 1 is 0.83, representing a strong linear correlation. In analyzing the data further, through a regression analysis, we calculate that the R^2, the coefficient of determination, was 68%. Therefore, 68% of the variation in 20-year annualized returns is explained by beginning year earnings yield. The equation of the line of best fit is: 20-year annualized return = 1.02 × (Earnings Yield) + 0.0307.

Observations of extreme high/low points of historical returns and earnings yields:

- The highest observed earnings yield of 13.7%, in 1975, produced a 14.33% annualized return.
- The lowest observed earnings yield of 4.54%, in 1998, produced a 7.11% annualized return.
- The highest observed 20-year portfolio return of 17.56% (1980–1999) began with an earnings yield of 13.51%.
- The lowest observed 20-year portfolio return of 6.42% (1959–1978) began with an earnings yield of 5.24%.
- Analyzing 2000–2017 (18 years): The beginning earnings yield in 2000 was 3.52% and the annualized return, over 18 years, is currently tracking at 5.34%. The 2000 vintage portfolio is on pace to produce a lower annualized return than any other vintage since 1957. Also, the 2000 vintage portfolio has the lowest starting earnings yield of any observed year since 1957.

Conclusions

Our conclusions from the analysis:

- A strong correlation exists between 20-year annualized returns of the S&P 500 and the beginning-of-period earnings yield.
- Much of the variation in 20-year annualized returns can be explained by beginning-of-period earnings yield.
- Beginning-of-period earnings yield provides a useful estimate of minimum expected return that investors can expect over a long-term horizon, specifically a 20-year investment period.

- Excess return above starting earnings yield is unexplained in this study when only using historical data available to an investor at the beginning of each period. We strongly suspect that forward earnings growth and/or inflation is the driver of the unexplained portion of the forward expected return.
- Long-term portfolio forecasting includes the mandate for investors to consider REAL (net of inflation returns). The nominal returns observed in this study provide a baseline from which investors can model for various forward-looking inflation scenarios.

Investors should use the earnings yield to approximate a minimum expected return for future financial planning. This conservative estimate of future returns could help reduce the unfunded liabilities that have accumulated in public pension plans due to poor forecasting. For individual investors, it should provide confidence that a minimum expected return can be achieved, even with unforeseen events, when investing over long-time horizons. In the practice of setting asset allocation policy, the use of earnings yield as a minimum expected return produces a more informed comparison of the future return potential of equities versus fixed income than the application of the theory of mean reversion or the Efficient Market Hypothesis.

References

Fama, E.F. "Random Walks in Stock Market Prices." *Financial Analysts Journal*, Vol. 21, No. 5 (1965), pp. 55–59.

Moody's Investors Service. "State and local government – U.S.: Pension burdens to rise through 2020, even in positive investment scenario." June 2017, https://www.moodys.com/research/Moodys-Pension-costs-will-rise-through-2020-even-in-best%2D%2DPR_368480.

The National Bureau of Economic Research. "U.S. Business Cycle Expansions and Contractions." 2017, http://www.nber.org/cycles/cyclesmain.html.

Siegel, Jeremy. *Stocks for the Long Run: The Definitive Guide to Financial Market Returns and Long-Term Investment Strategies (4th Edition)*. New York: McGraw-Hill, 2007. Print.

Silverblatt, H. "S&P Dow Jones Indices." 2017, http://us.spindices.com/indices/equity/sp-500.

8

Asset Allocation: Choices and Challenges

Asset allocation is the percentage of your portfolio that will be split between stocks, bonds, illiquid investments, and cash. A widely known academic study[1] concluded that it is the single most important determinant of the outcome of a portfolio's return over time. I fully agree. However, just because most investors and advisors focus on the asset allocation decision doesn't mean they get it right. It is not enough to allocate assets; you must make the RIGHT asset allocation decision!

Several generalizations about asset allocation have become conventional wisdom, accepted by many investors and advisors over the years. These over-simplifications have led many investors to err in constructing their portfolios and in what they expect the results to be. Among these over-simplifications are,

- Young investors with a 20+-year time horizon should own 100% equities and be impervious to portfolio volatility and the valuation of the equity markets.
- Workers who plan to retire in ten years or less should have an allocation equal to their age. (In other words, a 50-year-old should have 50% in bonds; a 70-year-old should have 70% in bonds; and so on.)
- Policy portfolios of 60% equity/40% bonds can be an alternative to a tactical allocation that requires paying attention to valuation and rebalancing.

---

[1] Brinson, Hood, and Beebower, "Determinants of Portfolio Performance" and Brinson, Hood, and Singer, "Determinants of Portfolio Performance II: An Update" in *Financial Analysts Journal*, 1986 and 1991.

© The Author(s) 2019
N. J. Gannon, *Tailored Wealth Management*,
https://doi.org/10.1007/978-3-319-99780-3_8

- Portfolios should be broadly diversified and include exposure to small, mid-, and large capitalization stocks, value and growth strategies, developed international companies, emerging markets companies, government bonds, corporate bonds, junk or high-yield bonds, managed futures, private equity (leveraged buyout), venture capital, currency trading, precious metals, and hedge funds.

Are these generalizations TRUE or FALSE? Not entirely true or false. Here's why.

Allocation Alone Is Not the Answer: Quality Counts

While there may be an element of historical correctness in a few of these statements, they prove to be dangerously false at specific points on the investment timeline. What is often lacking in these over-simplifications is that they do not include a minimum measure of quality for each of the assets in a portfolio. For example, they ignore such things as valuation, relative yield, and risk. Below are examples of several questions that must be asked:

- Should young investors be 100% invested in equities *no matter how overvalued*?
- Should young investors thumb their noses at a 13% 30-year government-guaranteed Treasury bond in favor of equities?
- Should 70-year-old retirees have 70% of their portfolios in bonds even if the yield on those bonds is negative (such as has been the case in the sovereign bonds of some European countries) or less than 1%?
- Should broadly diversified investors own thousands of stocks, bonds, currencies, metals, and funds without understanding any of them or without knowing whether they can provide a positive investment outcome?

When questions like these are asked in this way, it becomes clear that the investor MUST demand a minimum litmus test of quality, a line over which the strategy will not cross. For example, equity investors might place a valuation cap on their equity portfolio. In reviewing small capitalization and international stocks, they might study the relative value of these assets and (in the event they trade at a premium to US stocks) place a relative valuation cap of some pre-determined multiple of the P/E of the S&P 500 (or other relevant index). To do this effectively, investors must also understand how the P/E ratios of the indexes are calculated since different methods, set by the sponsor, are used by each index.

MarketWatch columnist Mark Hulbert wrote in August 2017 that the Russell 2000 Index of Small Capitalization Stocks was misleading investors because the way Russell calculates earnings per share for the index ignores companies with negative earnings. To illustrate the distortion, let's put it in personal terms using the example of a married couple. Mary, a general surgeon, earns an annual salary of $500,000. Her husband, Kevin, owns a chain of struggling neighborhood hardware stores that lost $100,000 in the previous calendar year. Logically, the annual income for the two nets Kevin's loss against Mary's wages for a combined annual income of $400,000. But using Russell's method for calculating earnings calculation, Kevin's loss would not be factored into the equation and Russell would set the combined wages for the couple at $500,000.

I use this example to highlight the importance of going beyond the published levels provided by the index sponsor or the financial media when analyzing P/E ratios. I would also pose the same challenge to index fund or exchange-traded fund (ETF) investors: either perform your own ongoing valuation analysis *or* simply ignore valuation yardsticks altogether.

When we review periods such as occurred in 2000, it becomes clear that ignoring P/E over-valuation has devastating consequences on portfolios. In a broader sense, limitations such as these in 2000, for example, would have kept portfolios from becoming over-exposed to over-valued stocks.

Similarly, fixed income investors might create a litmus test that prohibits them from investing in negative yielding government bonds (such as those offered in the European fixed income markets during the last decade).

In determining asset allocation and designing a diversified portfolio, investors should look to own assets for what they ARE as opposed to what they are NOT. It is not enough for investors to claim that they have obtained adequate portfolio diversification by adding high-yield bonds or hedge funds unless they have first determined whether those investments can claim a visible path to a successful long-term return as a stand-alone investment. For example, if high-yield (junk) bonds traded to a level of a 4% yield, the investor must subtract an expected default rate on the bonds (3 to 10%) as well as the effect of taxes. Since high-yield bonds were taxed as ordinary income, in 2017 a 4% portfolio could reasonably be expected to yield 2% or below net of taxes and defaults. High-yield bonds are indeed a diversifier within a portfolio, but I believe their benefit to the investor should be adjusted to account for their economic risk. Others believe that since broad diversification is the goal, increased exposure to asset classes (and managers within those asset classes) regardless of valuation or quality practices is warranted. I fervently disagree.

Asset Allocation by Type of Investor

Before exploring the reasons investors allocate assets the way they do, let's stop a moment to get a 50,000-foot view of what average allocations look like.

Family Office and College Endowment Investors

I have been an avid observer and participant in the Institute for Private Investors (IPI) Family Performance Tracking Survey and its more recent cousin, the Campden Global Family Office Survey. In writing this book, I reviewed the results of this survey over the past 21 years. Doing so gave me great insight into the gross and net returns of wealthy families' investment portfolios. I also examined the returns reported by the National Association of College and University Business Officers (NACUBO) survey, an institutional survey of how college endowments invest their capital (which includes portfolio allocations, performance, and spending policy), and was struck by the striking resemblance between the investing habits and asset allocations of these two groups. This was especially surprising because family portfolios can lose 25 to 50% of their investment returns to taxation.

According to the Campden Research Global Family Office Report 2017, across the family portfolios surveyed, the broad asset allocation mix was 48% alternative investments (hedge funds, private equity, real estate funds, managed futures funds, and other illiquid strategies), 27% equities, 15% bonds, 3% commodities, and 7% cash. (In Chap. 5 we discussed the impact fees can have on a portfolio. In this case, such a large allocation to alternative investments is a significant driver of the high fees paid by the average family office.)

When NACUBO released its 2017 survey results of college endowments, it showed alternative investments at 52%, global equities at 36%, bonds at 8%, and cash at 4%.

Comparing this allocation with the family office allocation above, you can see the striking parallel. Thus, despite the fact that some investors lose 50% of every unit of interest income, short-term capital gains, or hedge fund returns to taxes, Wall Street strategists continue to lump both groups into the same mold when it comes to asset allocation, completely ignoring the impact of taxes on the results; something college endowments do not face. Once again, risk and fees are amplified due to the high allocation to alternatives and illiquid investments.

Individual Investors

There is a difference between the needs of the do-it-yourself investor and the investor who works with an advisor. The former will need to subscribe to and be constantly informed about the changing relative value of the equity and bond markets. The latter will have outsourced this function and decision-making to the manager of their balanced mutual fund or their investment consultant. In either case, the investor should not and cannot outsource the task of understanding the raw materials of the portfolio, its ability to produce a positive return, or the relative safety of the assets in the capital structure.

Do-it-yourself investors have two options for setting and monitoring their asset allocation:

1. To maintain their own models for weighing the changing relative value of asset classes, or
2. To subscribe to an asset allocation program such as a robo-advisor or (on his own) mimic a large public investment portfolio such as CALpers or the NACUBO annual asset allocation survey.

Those who outsource their asset allocation have three options:

1. Employ an investment consultant who performs the asset allocation function and hires managers or funds to fill in the selected strategies, or
2. Select a balanced mutual fund where the tasks of asset allocation and security selection are performed by the same team (e.g., Dodge & Cox Balanced Fund [DODBX] or Vanguard Wellington Fund [VWELX]), or
3. Employ an outsourced Chief Investment Officer (CIO) who is responsible for both asset allocation and security selection.

In the following sections, I will examine the pros and cons of each method.

Do-It-Yourself Asset Allocation

It is rare to see a do-it-yourself investor who has built and maintained a sophisticated asset allocation model, spreadsheet, or software. It is more common for these investors to have drawn a conclusion (i.e., often not subject to debate) based upon personally selected traits of what a portfolio should and should not contain. For example, I have met corporate CEOs who had $50 to $100 million in assets when they retired who simply said, "On the day I retire, I am going to 100% bonds. End of story. I don't care if the yield is 1%, 5%, or 10%. I want 100% of my assets at the top of the capital structure, with a fixed rate of interest, and a guarantee of the return of my principal by the issuer at maturity. I don't care if the equity markets triple from today's prices. I understand that can occur, but I don't want to put my capital at risk."

It is hard to say this investor has made an uninformed decision. He feels that he has hedged against inflation as his assets grew from $5 million to $100 million; he has personal knowledge of the stock corrections that occurred along the way; and is unwilling to expose his post-retirement assets to equity volatility and risk. Fair enough. He has reasonably examined his appetite for risk and his willingness to forgo a more attractive (yet higher risk) portfolio return.

However, by deciding to exclusively own fixed income, this investor has subscribed to and exposed himself to risks that such investments cannot overcome, the most impactful of which are inflation risk, default risk, and interest rate risk. Investors with $100 million in high-grade municipal bonds in 2000 enjoyed $5 million in annual interest income from their portfolios. However, by 2017, they would have re-invested into bonds that yielded half that amount or less. While they were successful in achieving their goal of 100% fixed income, they willingly accepted the possibility that their portfolio yield could be reduced, in this example cut in half. Another possibility: Let's assume that these investors invested in a new portfolio yielding 2.5% and interest rates returned to a yield of 5%; the price of those bonds will be deeply (albeit temporarily) depressed until they reach par value at maturity or until interest rates drop again, *if* they drop again.

Just like our bond-favoring CEO, there are investors who declare that they will be 100% in stock no matter what. Believe it or not, one high net worth investor survey showed at least two families who maintained 100% of their portfolios in hedge funds. Obviously, these could have been anything from Elliott Management Company (a highly successful hedge fund managed by Paul Singer) to Madoff and everything in between.

Very early in my career, I had the opportunity to meet with a company founder who had recently sold his business for $100 million. I did not get the account. After interviewing several advisors, this investor (who had roughly $70 million after taxes) decided that he was going to buy $35 million in Berkshire Hathaway stock and put $35 million in the Vanguard S&P 500 index. Since the investment occurred close to the peak of the dot-com bubble in 2000, the S&P 500 under-performed his expectations by 50%, but the Berkshire Hathaway investment markedly out-performed. On balance, despite the "bet" he placed on the S&P 500, with the concentrated bet on the actively managed portfolio of the 70-something "Oracle of Omaha," he did alright.

One notable difference between this investor and most new retirees is that he did not need the income from the portfolio. All of it was invested for the benefit of his heirs after his death. Despite his success, I still believe this inves-tor took tremendous and unnecessary risks to achieve his goals. Picking one stock and one mutual fund could have had perilous results. Had he chosen WorldCom or Enron as his one stock or the Nasdaq 100 as his index fund, the portfolio would have been decimated—the stock went to zero and the "hot dot" index shed 50 to 75% of its value only two years into his investment.

Copycat Investors

There is an incredible amount of free information on the asset allocation hab-its of institutions. The Yale Endowment Annual Report (produced by famed investor David Swensen, CIO at Yale University) is a perfect specimen. For each of the past 15 years, Mr. Swensen reports the expected return of the endowment net of inflation. He provides details on the current allocation and targets of the endowment including the expected return on the sub-components of each asset class. It is written in layman's terms, without com-plexity and free of jargon. It is an informative read for anyone wishing to understand how to approach an asset allocation strategy.

For those who want to understand the imperative for a cause and effect relationship behind the goals of the asset allocation strategy, Mr. Swensen delivers. He tells you what he owns, why he owns it, and what he expects from each asset class. A simple Excel spreadsheet, to double check his math, reveals that the targeted return of the entire portfolio adds up when you combine the allocation targets and the expected return of each.

The NACUBO survey is a great source of asset allocation information. It is a compilation of the investment portfolios of hundreds of college endow-ments, and therefore represents the current status of big institutional portfo-lios. Sometimes the big money gets it right; sometimes they get it horribly wrong. It is important to know what the current thinking is at any point in time, whether you are looking to ride along or possibly take a contrarian approach. Yale and the University of Pennsylvania have managed to stay at the top of the survey. You will find the present observations of the most recent releases of these surveys in Table 8.1.

Copycats might be tempted to try to replicate the institutional portfolio with some passive version of their own. With public company equities, this is easily accomplished through passive vehicles. Challenges arise, however, when you consider the fact that taxes matter to the individual and do not to the endowment investor. In the hedge fund world, high-turnover strategies, which may produce positive fee adjusted results, may fail the test once the tax

Table 8.1 Allocations for wealthy families and institutions

Asset	IPI/Campden	NACUBO
Fixed income	15	8
Public equities	27	36
Venture capital	9	6
Private equity	7	12
Co-investing	4	
Real estate and REITS	17	6
Hedge funds	6	19
Other	3	2
ETFs	2	
Commodities	3	7
Cash or equivalent	7	4
Total	100	100

bite is factored in. In the private equity space, a retail investor will not have access to the deals that Yale and Wharton see, and, in many cases, the result will be a watered-down investment product producing mediocre results.

Balanced Mutual Fund Investors

Investors who select a balanced mutual fund are hiring the fund as both manager and asset allocator, and, for this reason, must do their homework as part of the selection process. Small investors, and even large ones, can succeed by having all or a substantial portion of their portfolio in one such fund. It is a very short list, but investors can find funds with 25-, even 75-, year track records that have invested through the major booms and busts of recent history. Investors can benefit from studying these funds to see how they were positioned at peaks and troughs of markets. In this way, they can see, for example, whether the funds correctly increased their allocation to fixed income in 1981, 2000, or 2007. They can view webcasts of interviews with the portfolio management team who are eager to discuss their mistakes as well as their successes.

Investors should look for firms that have an articulated ethos about the way they manage money and the way they see their role as a steward of client assets. These firms should have a deep bench of investment talent and should not overly rely on the skills of one individual. In this way, the investment process is more likely to be repeatable.

In addition, if the fund's sponsor is employee owned rather than controlled by a single family, there is less risk of a "cash out" event with the sale of the firm. While this is in no way a recommendation, DODBX and VWELX are two that warrant the smaller investors' attention. Wellington began in July 1929. What a terrible time to begin a fund! They did an admirable job making decisions on asset allocation and security selection for their shareholders at a time when many portfolios vanished as a result of poor decision-making.

The Investment Consultant as Asset Allocator

Many large family portfolios are served by an investment consultant who charges a fee to construct and implement an investment policy statement, provide asset allocation recommendations, and select money managers to perform a specific role in the diversified portfolio. This model is by far the most widely practiced in the ultra-high net worth space as it offers both active and passive strategies, keeps the consultant agnostic on the selection of managers (his compensation is unrelated to his choices), and offers the investor an orchestra conductor who has eyes on all corners of the portfolio.

There are many skilled practitioners of the consulting model available to investors today. There are also a large number of consultants who tend to gravitate around the "norms" of the day, not wanting to express a bias for or against any asset class. What can happen in these cases is that portfolios become overly diversified or imbalanced at market tops when valuations swell. Such strategies did not work out well in 2008 and 2009 because the diversification effect, which was supposed to be achieved by investing in non-US-based assets, failed when the financial crisis spread to other corners of the globe.

The best consultants in the industry are proud of the uniqueness of their thinking and are more than eager to show why they made deliberate shifts in search of safety or opportunity. Those that have demonstrated long-term success AND a strategy that is convincingly repeatable are the ones that should make the short list for investors looking to hire a consultant.

Dual-Role Asset Allocator and Manager

The largest segment of the investing population using this model are large institutions with a deep in-house team that self-selects its asset allocation strategy and most, if not all, portfolio management tasks. Yale Endowment is a good example of this, although Yale continues to selectively evaluate and outsource alternative investment management opportunities. Another segment of investors who perform the dual role are large $1+ billion family offices. A CIO is charged with the task of designing the asset mix and managing individual illiquid investments. The CIO may be served by an in-house portfolio management team for sourcing individual ideas.

The smallest segment of the dual-role manager is the one I am most familiar with. I refer to it as the outsourced CIO model; a concentrated team of investment professionals charged with the task of setting asset allocation policy, implementing it within client portfolios, and selecting individual securities within the portfolio. There is much similarity between the outsourced CIO and the balanced mutual fund manager. The main difference is that the CIO directly buys investments for each family portfolio he manages whereas the balanced fund manager manages one multibillion dollar account which is sub-divided into mutual fund shares for its constituents. One benefit CIOs have that the fund managers do not is that that they own an individual portfolio of individual securities that will not be affected by the liquidity crunches that face mutual funds and ETFs during periods of amplified volatility. The CIO is also able to exclude certain securities from a family portfolio and even accept input from the family on proxy voting issues.

I would like to see an increase in the number of outsourced CIO managers. While well managed balanced mutual funds exist, the open-end mutual fund structure is inappropriate for large taxable portfolios that need individualized tax management, tax-exempt fixed income, and protection from forced liquidations caused by other shareholders.

Deciding How to Invest: Do-It-Yourself versus Funds versus Financial Advisor

For investors choosing to outsource the task of asset allocation and security selection to a professional, I strongly suggest that they select a balanced global strategy where the manager has the discretion to own equities and fixed income in a coordinated effort. When you find a fund with a repeatable process or ethos that governs the portfolio, you won't have to worry when one member of the investment team retires or leaves the firm.

Do-it-yourself investors must immerse themselves in the finer points of investing, which includes:

- Evaluating the relative value between the equity and bond markets. They will need that for the first asset allocation decision.
- Knowing how to look for periods when the equity risk premium goes negative, prompting the decision to overweight bonds, and then, when conditions warrant, deciding to reverse this stance.
- Ascertaining the relative valuation of the major world economies and their stock markets and currency.
- Understanding the various methodologies for calculating qualitative metrics such as P/E ratios or book value that are used by different index sponsors such as Standard & Poor's, Russell, and others.
- Determining whether their chosen index fund strategy will be market capitalization weighted or equal weighted. The capitalization weighted index weights the companies in the index by their size or market capitalization. In this scenario, the dollars allocated to Google will dwarf those allocated to a company like Big Lots. In an equal weighted fund each of the companies in the index receives the same amount of investment dollars.

Do-it-yourself investors will need to optimize their decisions on all of these inflection points, and should take their time and study these important topics before putting a single dollar at risk. This may seem like a lot for the individual investor to shoulder, but some have the temperament and knowledge to succeed doing it this way. To quote the iconic Canadian rock band Rush, "If you choose not to decide you still have made a choice."

For investors choosing to go with a financial advisor, there are two things that are critical to your success: (1) finding an advisor with whom you have a genuine chemistry, one with whom you feel you will be able to build a relationship, and (2) choosing an advisor who is able to explain in language that *you* understand how they intend to protect and build your capital. Early in the process, it is very easy to meet someone and immediately trust them. Resist the temptation. Do your due diligence. TAKE YOUR TIME in formulating your plan. This is especially important for those of you who are recently divorced or have lost the spouse who made a majority of financial decisions.

Make sure to ask the advisor about their mother's portfolio—what it is invested in, whether she has a mortgage or not. A very easy question to ask of the advisor: "At what interest rate would you advise me to put my entire portfolio into treasury bonds or FDIC insured CDs?" There must be a number where every investor or advisor says to themselves, "If I could earn _____ in low-risk, long-term bonds I would do it." You'll get interesting answers to this question when interviewing potential candidates.

A financial advisor may be the highest-paid person in your annual budget. You must understand whether the fees they charge add value. It is also important for you to be able to delineate the fees that go toward straight money management versus those that compensate your advisor for her time and financial planning. Too often, the advisor hides behind low-fee index funds or ETFs and marries the strategy with an expensive financial planning fee. It is perfectly reasonable for you to compensate your advisor; just don't over-pay and certainly don't over-pay to the point where net portfolio returns are challenged. The advisors who made billions in fees while the pension fund shortfall ballooned to $4 trillion certainly did not give their clients their money's worth.

9

Defining Moment: Your Objectives, Assumptions, and Other Factors Affecting Long-Term Returns

According to the June 8, 2018, release from the US Federal Reserve,[1] the combined unfunded liability of private and public pension funds stood at $3.9 trillion. This stunning failure to fund the future of many American retirees was avoidable.

Several decades before the under-funding of pension funds manifested itself, many wealth managers and pension consultants believed that a 60% equity/40% bond portfolio OR a widely diversified portfolio of various asset classes could achieve "average" long-term results of 8 or 9%. In the last two decades of the 1980s and 1990s this was an achievable goal, but remember that in 1981, long-term treasury bond yields were 13% and stock P/E ratios stood at seven times (an earnings yield of 14%). Thus, it was reasonable to assume that a portfolio blend of these two assets could easily achieve a 20-year return north of 9% even after fees.

Fast forward to the year 2000: On January 1, 2000, a 20-year US Treasury bond yielded 6% (less than half of its yield in 1981) and stock P/E multiples had risen to 28 times (an earnings yield of 3.57%). Therefore, if bonds simply earned their yield to maturity of 6% and equities earned their earnings yield plus inflation, it would be mathematically impossible for the portfolio to achieve the 8 or 9% return that was possible in the 20-year period beginning in 1981.

Yet, instead of acknowledging the failure of "mean reversion," some in the investment community (including those in charge of $20 trillion in US

---

[1] https://www.federalreserve.gov/releases/z1/current/.

© The Author(s) 2019
N. J. Gannon, *Tailored Wealth Management*,
https://doi.org/10.1007/978-3-319-99780-3_9

pension assets) still believe that once a long-term historical trend is observed, that trend will drive future returns in such a way that the long-term trend will be upheld. Whether it was optimism or some other theory or belief that led to the $3.9 trillion under-funding of pension funds, the lesson does not seem to have been learned. Institutional investors have not changed their strategy quickly enough and continue to march along to the same drumbeat under the banner of hope.

Throughout this book, I have cautioned investors about the dangers of making "long-term" assumptions about the potential of various investments based upon backward-looking data points. The massive pension shortfall is a perfect illustration of the dangers that lurk behind such a strategy. When you compare the actuarial assumptions behind the pension funds' long-term investment strategy forecast, the reason for their performance is clear: those assumptions were mathematically impossible to achieve during the last two decades, which saw higher stock valuations and lower interest rates than their forecasts anticipated.

Pension fund sponsors were not the only ones who experienced lower portfolio results than expected over the last two decades. Even when top-line results appear to have been successful, once the effect of portfolio taxation, spending, and inflation is taken into account, many funds produced zero or even negative real results.

Table 9.1 is an analysis of portfolio returns and net worth using four benchmarks. The first is the IPI/Campden family performance tracking survey[2] of the world's wealthiest families who report annually on their portfolio asset allocation and performance. The second is the NACUBO survey of the largest college endowments. US Household Net Worth, the third benchmark, is the quarterly report from the Federal Reserve that accumulates the aggregate wealth of American households and non-profit corporations. Last, the Forbes 400 list of the richest Americans is included as a measure of the annual growth in net worth necessary for the 400th member of the list to *stay* on the list.

For the purpose of comparison, for both IPI and NACUBO data, I used gross investment returns, and then applied a tax adjustment to both to come up with estimated after-tax portfolio returns. Although the college endowment portfolios are essentially free from portfolio taxation, I made the tax

---

[2] Institute for Private Investors (subsidiary of Campden Wealth) Family Performance Tracking Survey, 1997–2014. 2015–2017 data sourced from Campden Global Family Office Report published by Campden Research. Data for 2017 lacked a usable data set for family office performance. For 2017 I used the ratio of the IPI/Campden to NACUBO annualized returns from 1997 to 2006, which resulted in an assumed performance of 1.06 times the NACUBO return for 2017 (IPI/Campden 7.18%/NACUBO 6.75% = 1.06 times).

Table 9.1 Average portfolio returns 1997–2017

Year	IPI	NACUBO[1]	US net worth	Forbes 400
1997	20.00%	20.40%	11.03%	14.46%
1998	8.00%	18.00%	11.07%	5.26%
1999	18.00%	11.00%	12.50%	25.00%
2000	8.50%	13.00%	1.47%	16.00%
2001	−3.00%	−3.60%	1.01%	−17.24%
2002	−6.40%	−6.00%	−1.13%	−8.33%
2003	17.50%	3.00%	12.28%	9.09%
2004	11.00%	15.10%	14.32%	25.00%
2005	10.00%	9.30%	10.96%	20.00%
2006	12.30%	10.70%	6.94%	11.11%
2007	12.40%	17.20%	0.46%	30.00%
2008	−25.00%	−3.00%	−15.50%	0.00%
2009	17.27%	−18.70%	3.14%	−26.15%
2010	11.26%	11.90%	7.16%	4.17%
2011	0.21%	19.20%	2.08%	5.00%
2012	10.00%	−0.30%	9.23%	4.76%
2013	17.00%	11.70%	13.96%	18.18%
2014	8.34%	15.50%	6.31%	19.23%
2015	0.30%	2.40%	4.06%	9.68%
2016	7.00%	−1.90%	6.32%	0.00%
2017	12.93%	12.20%	7.82%	17.65%
Annualized return	**7.45%**	**7.00%**	**5.75%**	**7.78%**
*A/T retention**	0.78	0.78	1	1
After tax return	**5.81%**	**5.46%**	**5.75%**	**7.78%**
*Spending rate***	4.00%	4.37%	0.00%	0.00%
*Inflation****	2.20%	2.20%	2.20%	2.20%
After tax, spending, & inflation return	**−0.39%**	**−1.11%**	**3.55%**	**5.58%**

IPI Institute for Private Investors Annual Family Performance Tracking Survey With Private Equity—Ultra-high net worth investor survey that highlights returns and asset allocations of IPI member families. IPI member families have minimum assets of $30 million. The returns with private equity include an adjustment to 2008 when it was reported that private equity returns were 0%. A negative return adjustment was made to account for a negative return from private equity allocation. IPI survey results were used for years 1997-2014. The Global Family Office Report from Campden Research (IPI's parent company) was used for 2015 and 2016. No results were available for 2017 so we have implied an estimated return using a 20-year annualized return comparison between IPI/Campden and NACUBO (IPI/Campden 7.18%/NACUBO 6.75%=1.06x). Thus, the IPI/Campden return used for 2017 is 1.06x that of NACUBO's 2017 return.

NACUBO The National Association of College and University Business Officers (NACUBO) is a membership organization representing more than 2500 colleges, universities, and higher education service providers across the country and around the world. Commonfund Study of Endowments (NCSE) final report includes information gathered from the endowments and affiliated foundations of 835 US colleges and universities, representing total endowment assets of $448 billion.[1] Returns have year ends of June 30

(*continued*)

Table 9.1 (continued)

US net worth Households and Nonprofit Organizations; Net Worth, Not Seasonally Adjusted Data. The US Net Worth data is pulled from the Federal Reserve Bank of St. Louis, FRED system (Federal Reserve Economic Data). This data represents the level of net worth (balance sheets) of US Households and Nonprofit Organizations

Forbes 400 Data represents the year-over-year change in the net worth of the 400th individual listed on the Forbes 400. The Forbes 400, compiled annually, is a list of the richest US individuals

*A/T retention IPI & NACUBO were assumed to have a 78% after-tax retention rate. The pre-liquidation after-tax return for IPI was reported at 78% according to their 2014 report

**Spending rate IPI & NACUBO average spending rates from 1997 to 2017. US net worth and Forbes 400 returns are reported net of spending

***Inflation Average annual CPI rate of 2.2% from 1997 to 2017. Data sourced from the US Bureau of Labor Statistics

adjustment to illustrate what a family would achieve if investing their portfolio exactly in line with the NACUBO mix. The US household net worth and the Forbes 400 data are provided to demonstrate how these returns compare to the others. These figures are also *net* of taxes and spending (normal living expenses and gifts to family members), since we are measuring aggregate net worth from January 1 to December 31 of each year.

For the period observed, the IPI/Campden survey showed a pre-tax portfolio return of 7.45% and an after-tax return of 5.81% (after-tax retention rate of 78%). This net return is only 29 basis points better than a home state 20-year non-callable tax-free municipal bond in 1997 (as evidenced by the average yield of the *Bond Buyer 20 Index of General Obligation* bonds). The heavy allocation to alternative investments, including hedge funds, did not provide a material long-term portfolio out-performance especially if you consider the increased risk as well as the fees paid by investors to do so.

The NACUBO results show a similar lack of a reasonable risk premium: for the period observed, the NACUBO endowments produced a 7% return (untaxed), yet this result is only a 31 basis point annualized premium over the 6.69% yield on a 20-year US Treasury bond (the average yield for 1997).[3]

Note: The IPI/Campden and NACUBO surveys represent gross portfolio results before spending or distributions. If we assume that the average wealthy family and college endowment exhibited a 4 to 4.5% spending policy, then net results (after distributions) would be reduced to 2 to 3% over these 21 years.

---

[3] Those who wish to study the NACUBO data in greater detail should note that this survey uses a June 30 calendar year end reporting period. Thus, in any given year, users should avoid drawing conclusions on the dispersion between NACUBO and the other three benchmarks (which report on the calendar year). The aggregated compounded annual growth rate is a reliable data point since in the 21 years of this study 246 out of 252 months will be common to all four benchmarks.

Notice that the average US household (showing 5.75% 21-year increase in net worth) actually grew faster than the average wealthy family's or the average college endowment did.

If risk is supposed to compensate the investor with additional return over time, over the past two decades, the results have not lived up to the promise of this axiom. Perhaps, the alarm has sounded its warning that status quo portfolio strategy is in need of reform.

These results should come as no surprise to investors, especially in light of the trillions of dollars of under-funded pensions that exist for the very same reason. My advice for both taxable and institutional investors is to study these numbers and ask themselves what drove the decisions to allocate assets the way they did in each of those years. Where they chose to increase equity, hedge fund, or private equity risk, what assumptions were used that drove forward-looking portfolio forecasts? Where riskier portfolios were constructed that failed to produce a meaningful risk premium, how can decisions in the future be made such that the investor can be reasonably assured of not repeating this mistake?

Our Efficient Valuation Hypothesis[4] and 2006 after-tax study gave insights at the beginning of each year into whether investors were being compensated for risk. It demonstrated that those who understood the relationship between P/Es and interest rates meaningfully out-performed those who hoped for a reversion to historically observed capital markets compounding rates. Investors can do better. For this reason, I'm calling for a new debate about how they can tighten their shot pattern and improve results and portfolio forecasts.

Impact of Taxes on Portfolio Returns

Note that portfolio taxation takes a tremendous toll on a taxable portfolio as represented by the IPI benchmark. For the 21 years from 1997 to 2017 this group, on average, achieved a 7.45% annualized return gross of taxes. However, due to the taxation of interest, dividends, capital gains, and hedge funds, they achieved an after-tax retention rate of 78%, leaving only 5.81% net of taxes. When factoring in an average spending rate of 4%, the net of tax and spending return drops to 1.81%. Over the same period, the Consumer Price Index (CPI) averaged 2.2%, meaning that REAL results (after inflation) were −0.39%. As Table 9.1 demonstrates, the average wealthy family portfolio over the last 21 years lost ground net of taxes, spending, and inflation. This is a stark reality and, as the adage goes, the proof is in the pudding; the status

---

[4] Niall J. Gannon and Scott B. Seibert, CFA, "Forecasting Portfolio Returns: The Efficient Valuation Hypothesis" Seeking Alpha, March 6, 2018.

quo has simply not been good enough. Wealth management firms who advertised that they would preserve the lifestyle of the family across the generations proved that they weren't able to do so for the first generation.

What could be done to improve results for investors? An understanding of the Efficient Valuation Hypothesis would help investors obtain better and more accurate long-term portfolio results. It would, for example, have better protected do-it-yourself investors' capital at the peak of the 2000 dot-com bubble. You may recall from Chap. 7 that when the P/E ratio of US stocks pierced through 30 times between January and March 2000, it was a signal that this asset class was priced to under-perform high-grade municipal bonds for the subsequent 20-years. Those who observed this point when the equity risk premium went negative (meaning the expected return on stocks was less than the expected return on bonds) would have decreased equity allocations and increased bond allocations.

In writing this book, I looked at the NACUBO asset allocation survey from 2000, and observed that fixed income allocations came to approximately 23% which, in my view, means that these investors chose to maintain an equity and risk over-weight posture without a valuation justification for doing so. I can only conclude that the theory of mean reversion was so deeply rooted among institutional investors (including the NACUBO endowments) they thought they could pay no attention to the price of the assets they were buying and nevertheless continue to earn the average returns they had been receiving.

College endowments, as represented by the NACUBO survey, did a little worse than the IPI group at 7% annualized over the past 21 years. However, college endowments enjoy the benefit of a non-taxed portfolio, thus they did not cede 22% of their investment return to taxes as the IPI group did. However, the NACUBO survey reported an average spending policy of 4.37% per year,[5] dropping their net of spending portfolio results to 2.63%. Subtracting the 2.2% CPI from the NACUBO group left *real* results net of spending and inflation to only 0.48%. The College Board reported in 2015 that the previous ten-year inflation rate on college tuition was approximately 5% annually. If the NACUBO group adjusts for the rate of college tuition cost inflation (rather than the CPI which measures the rate of inflation across the entire economy), then the NACUBO group also experienced a negative REAL rate of return: 2.63% annualized portfolio return net of spending minus 5% college tuition inflation means the endowment *lost* 2.37% in real terms.

---

[5] 2017 NACUBO-Commonfund Study of Endowments® (NCSE).

Strategies to Enhance Returns

In the spring of 2006, Vanguard chairman Jack Bogle addressed the IPI Spring Forum in New York and suggested that the group's portfolios had become too complex suggesting that the heavy reliance on hedge funds, high-yield bonds, real estate, private equity, venture capital, and managed futures funds produced a high-fee alternative to Vanguard's own (actively managed) Wellington balanced mutual fund. Bogle surmised that if investors simply invested in this one fund (in which he argued they would receive adequate diversification among asset classes, geographic regions, and individual securities), they would achieve a superior net return than they were receiving at the time from their investing strategy. A Morningstar hypothetical illustration that compares Wellington (ticker VWELX) or Dodge & Cox Balanced (ticker DODBX) over the same 21 years of the study confirms that Bogle was justified in his assessment.

Even though these two funds are considered tax inefficient (in that they own taxable rather than tax-exempt bonds), their gross results in the hypothetical illustration suggest the two funds would have out-performed the IPI benchmark by 77 basis points (annualized) for Wellington and 137 basis points (annualized) for Dodge & Cox. In addition, their out-performance holds up on a net of tax basis and takes this group of investors from a negative real rate of return to a positive one.

While I have never personally invested in either of these two funds, it is clear that our ability to out-perform these investor and institutional benchmarks—the effect—was a result of practicing a value-driven asset allocation overlay with an actively managed portfolio of global businesses and bonds—the cause. I should note that an open-end mutual fund structure under which the Wellington and Dodge & Cox funds exist is inappropriate for a wealthy family with more than $5 million due to their tax inefficiency, the loss of individual tax lot control, inherited embedded capital gains, and the risk of liquidity runs on the fund. However, the performance shown in the Morningstar hypotheticals speaks to the success of the underlying strategy employed by the portfolio managers.

The out-performance of the balanced strategy is borne out by the results of the NACUBO survey. The two balanced funds (VWELX and DODBX) out-performed the NACUBO benchmark by an even wider margin—163 basis points and 204 basis points respectively—from 1997 to 2017. Further out-performance could have been achieved by the taxable portfolios had they simply adapted the fixed income allocation to a tax-exempt bond instead of a taxable bond sub-strategy, a practice I have personally used throughout my career. In examining the results of the NACUBO survey, it should be noted that a small number of endowments managed to practice an effective asset allocation, eschewed alternative investments and passive index funds, and produced attractive results using a simple mix of actively managed stocks and individual fixed income investments. In another tip of the hat to a simple versus a complex portfolio strategy, a June 25, 2018, article in the *Wall Street Journal* highlighted the success of Quinnipiac University's investment team (who completely eschew investments in index funds, ETF's and alternative investments), noting their returns for the decade ended June 30, 2017, were in the top 10% of the endowments ranked by the NACUBO survey.

Factors to Consider

Investors should not feel that they need 10 or 15 investment managers, funds, or ETFs with exposure to thousands of individual securities if this practice has failed to reduce risk or produce excess return. The results of the Quinnipiac, Wellington, and Dodge & Cox portfolios provide the proof. There are a handful of other managers nationally who will construct a balanced, tax-efficient, actively managed strategy that can support their performance skill with a Global Investment Performance Standards audited and verified track record. These firms should be considered when a family is considering hiring or replacing its primary financial advisor.

When reviewing the data in Table 9.1, the growth in the mean net worth of the American household not only looks good, it is stellar. The average US household actually out-performed the family offices (IPI/Campden) and the college endowments (NACUBO). The US Household Net Worth figure, as we noted above, is net of all portfolio spending, fees, and taxes. Thus 5.37% annualized growth rate need only be reduced by the 2.2% CPI to produce a REAL return of 3.17%. The main difference between the IPI private investor survey and the average US family is that the former likely depends on portfolio distributions to fund annual living expenses whereas the latter uses earned income and thus are net contributors to their assets. Another difference, although less impactful, is that the tax code immediately affects the wealthy investors' portfolio at the top rates whereas the average US family generally enjoys a lower net tax rate and long-term tax deferral on qualified retirement plan and pension assets.

The 21-year performance data presented in Table 9.1 also highlights another surprising outcome. Comparing the net of spending and inflation results between the average US household and the Forbes 400 the spread is not as wide as you might think. This is because the rate of inflation on Forbes 400 family expenditures is different from that of the typical household. *Forbes* magazine has been computing a luxury rate of inflation back to the very first Forbes 400 list in 1982. The CLEWI (Cost of Living Extremely Well Index) measures the price inflation on luxury goods and services. For example, it includes the annual price change of an Ebony concert-grand Steinway piano, a 75-foot Hatteras motor yacht, the average price of a thoroughbred yearling at the Keenland, Kentucky, September sale, a Russian sable fur coat from Bloomingdale's, horsebit leather loafers from Gucci, and a case of current vintage Dom Pérignon champagne. In the November 14, 2017, issue of *Forbes*, the editors reported that since the inception of the index the average price increase in the CLEWI was 5% per year compared to the CPI at approximately 3%. Subtracting the 5% luxury index from the Forbes 400 leaves this group with a 2.78% REAL return, roughly in line with the real return of the average US household.

Different Strokes for Different Goals

The exercise of tracking portfolio returns net of fees, taxes, spending, and inflation yields this very obvious takeaway: portfolios designed for different objectives should be approached, built, monitored, and managed in completely independent ways that maximize the NET outcome for each. If your investment consultant's recommended allocation looks remarkably similar to that of the typical college endowment, something is terribly wrong.

The Role of Long-Term Assumptions on Objectives

In *Investing Strategies*, I discussed the markedly altered risk/reward equation that affects investors who pay taxes at the top brackets on portfolio gains. Since then I have addressed groups of non-taxable investors, such as those who advise pension plan administrators, and have been surprised to find how few of them realized or understood the role the risk/reward equation and their failure to adapt to changes in the marketplace played in their inability to achieve their long-term assumptions.

In pension accounting (and, to some degree, in individual investing), the higher you assume your investment return will be, the less money you need to invest today. As discussed in detail at the beginning of this chapter, in the last decades of the twentieth century, many wealth managers and pension consultants believed that they could achieve "average" long-term results of 8 or 9%. For a time they were not wrong. Unrealistically high return assumptions were kind to the immediate bottom line of corporations and government entities that minimized the dollars they contributed to pension plans assuming future lofty returns would bail them out.

Sadly, those results were no longer possible in the first decades of the twenty-first century, yet many continued to invest as if it was, and the result, as we have seen, is a $3.9 trillion shortfall. It should be noted that the bulk of that deficit exists in the pension funds of federal government employees as well as state and local governments. Corporate pension plans have been better managed in that shortfalls from the investment portfolio have been buttressed by cash payments from the parent corporations to keep the funding level on track. Federal, state, and local governments have largely ignored their funding problems and have allowed the deficits to pile up (note this continued to happen during the nine-year bull market from 2009 to 2017).

Planning based solely on conservative return assumptions has a cost, which is that your ending portfolio value will be smaller than if you had created a plan that contained some rosy assumptions. I believe that investors should expose themselves to assets that *may* benefit from upside surprises, but the plan itself should not assume these surprises will occur. So think and act on the belief that you'll end up with a conservative return, and if you get the benefit of P/E expansion (such as was witnessed from 1996 to 2000) your portfolio will participate.

The investors with the most predictable returns are those with the lowest long-term return assumptions, and that group is comprised of those whose portfolios contain 100% bonds or fixed income. This group thumbs its nose at upside surprises, hedges against inflation, and ignores the booms that come from equity bull markets.

As our 21-year illustration shows, investors in 1997 could buy a 20-year treasury bond with a yield to maturity of 6.69%. At that moment, the S&P 500 was trading at an earnings yield of 5.49%, but there was always the possibility that it could benefit from some unknown upside earnings surprise or P/E multiple expansion. A bond investor could have weighed the two options and said, "6.69% treasuries (or 5.6% tax exempt municipal bonds) is good enough for me. I can spend my coupon and, assuming the US treasury doesn't default, I'll get my principal back in 20 years." We should never forget that only one month prior to January 1997, Fed Chairman Alan Greenspan famously cautioned that the US equity market was beginning to exhibit "irrational exuberance." That may well have given bond investors at least some measure of intellectual support for their decision to earn a finite and predictable 6.6% return. Although *Stocks for the Long Run* and *The Great Boom Ahead* were bestselling books at the time, bond investors were happy to allow those who took more risk to earn more if time proved those authors correct.

What happened to our bond investors? They earned 6.6% from their taxable treasuries or 5.6% from their tax-exempt municipal bonds and their principal was returned to them when the bonds expired. They performed remarkably well, quite happy with the fact that investors who took much more risk in equities, hedge funds, or alternative investments didn't do much better after fees and taxes. The NACUBO portfolio, achieving gross returns of 7%, was only 31 basis points higher than the treasury bond. When you consider that the treasury bond could have been purchased at the auction window with no fee, put the investor at the very top of the capital structure, and provided an exact and predictable cash flow in each and every year, you can only conclude that the NACUBO portfolio paid a lot of fees and took a tremendous amount of risk to achieve only an additional 31 basis points in return.

Am I arguing that a bond portfolio is superior to a complex, broadly diversified portfolio containing riskier assets? Absolutely not! One can answer that question only when measuring and comparing the forward expected returns on all asset classes. What's more there are certain risks that bond investors take and they should be acknowledged. So, here's the challenge for the bond investor: the yield (2.6%) on NEW 20-year treasury bonds at year end 2017 was less than half the yield on the bonds in a portfolio that had recently matured. Since then, the cost of living has risen somewhat, so in addition to the yield being cut in half, those dollars will buy less than what they could have bought in 1997. As a result, bond investors now find themselves at a new inflection point. Choice A is to simply accept the yield of the bond market, cut their annual expenses by more than 50%, and continue to invest as a passive consumer of whatever the treasury or municipal bond market is paying at the time their bonds mature.

But, bond investors do have another option, Choice B; they could do the interest rate/earnings yield comparison once more. If they do this (as of this writing, June 2018), they will see that they can buy a portfolio of globally diversified businesses (stocks) with an earnings yield of 5% for 60% of their portfolio and balance this with a much smaller treasury or municipal bond allocation of 40%. This gross tax blend offers them a minimum expected return of around 4%. The return on their fixed income portfolio will be predictable over the next 20 years and their equity portfolio should produce at least its earnings yield.

Since in most long-term business cycles, a portfolio of businesses (stocks) will also experience the earnings growth of its net income, the equity portfolio has the potential for the long-term return to rise from 5 to 6 or 7%. Four percent is a commonly quoted "prudent" portfolio spending rate used by financial planners and wealth managers, so in choosing such a portfolio and capping their spending rate at 4%, investors have not fallen victim to rosy assumptions.

When the Federal Reserve began its policy of quantitative easing coming out of the 2008 financial crisis, it fully intended to push investors out of safer investments like bank deposits, certificates of deposits, or bonds and into riskier assets such as real estate and equities. While American households still hold over $10 trillion in cash and short-term securities,[6] the Fed certainly got its way and brought many investors into the stock market simply because they ran out of options at the banks and in the bond market.

On the investment front, no matter where you fall on the active versus passive debate or whether you wish to be all stocks or all bonds: DECLARE YOUR MAJOR. This decision is way too important to wing it. Decide for yourself what the causes of portfolio success are, examine the effects these may have, revisit the allocation once a year, and keep climbing.

The Impact of Your Time Horizon on Your Investment Strategy

As you may have guessed, I am a fan of using 20-year time horizons to define "long term." In Chap. 7, I discussed the rolling 20-year periods from 1957 to the present, and pointed out the strong correlation between actual returns and the interest rates and earnings yields at the time of purchase. Ten years seems to me too short a timeframe, since bubbles can form within the decade, crash toward the end, and leave the investor with a loss that was not foreseeable at the portfolio's inception. For this reason, it is prudent that when you know you will have to withdraw money from your portfolio within three years, a good rule of thumb is to migrate those funds out of your long-term investment strategy.

For workers under the age of 30 with a 401k and a long-time horizon: Begin with this in mind: The amount that you put INTO your portfolio is more important than how much you earn FROM your portfolio. Again, the concept of being a rabid saver comes into play; I would rather see you max

---

[6] Board of Governors of the Federal Reserve System, *Financial Accounts of the United States*, Second Quarter, 2017.

your savings rate and own a mediocre fund than have you contribute only a modest amount such as 5 to 10% to your 401k. I say that about mediocre funds because more important than the fund to the outcome is the amount you invest. The tortoise who saves more will pass the hare who invests less, not only in the value of his portfolio, but also because if he spends his days focused on his job instead of on the pile of money he will have when he quits his job, he will earn more and have more to invest.

Therefore, invest the maximum allowed contribution and weight your portfolio with a globally diversified portfolio of companies. If an actively managed option is available in your 401k, study the fund, its management team, and fees and make an informed decision. Many people in this age group may find the siren song of easy money in index funds hard to resist. While I won't re-argue that case here, if you choose this route, it's important to make sure that you keep watch in the tower for the pitfalls that have taken 50 to 80% of investor capital over the last few decades.

For middle-aged workers and a medium time horizon: For those approaching 50, it's time to start evaluating the role that fixed income might play in your portfolio, not only because of the increased yield but for the surety of return. As mentioned earlier in the chapter, bonds must, just like any other asset, be viewed in terms of their risk and reward. At the end of 2017 there were sovereign bonds of European countries trading at a negative yield. This is an example of an unmatched case of risk and reward. Therefore, at this point in your investing life, when putting together a fixed income portfolio, it is important to assess the quality, return potential, and inherent risk of the securities in the portfolio.

At this point, too, you may be attracted to "packaged" investment products such as annuities, unit trusts, or funds. It is important to note here that packaged products do not open you up to new opportunities. Therefore, it is important not to view these products as investments. An annuity (issued by an insurance company) is backed by a separate account (managed by the sponsoring insurance company) and can only select from the same securities as everyone else in the world. Packaged investment products, in comparison to separately managed accounts, are targeted toward investors who are unlikely to peel back the onion. In this respect, they are similar to a mutual fund or unit trust. In addition, annuities assess mortality charges and distribution fees in order to fund death benefits and the insurance component of the contract. Some annuities contain a death benefit guarantee that is attractive to the annuitant. Investors should realize that these products, which combine liquid securities, life insurance, and internally managed derivatives, are only as good as the underlying assets less their fees. The yield or death benefit should not be your primary consideration when purchasing an annuity. Peel back the onion and understand how they plan to meet their obligation to you. There are cases, however, where an annuity contract can offer a guaranteed death benefit for an older investor who would otherwise be unwilling to subject her portfolio to daily volatility.

What to Do When All Your Eggs Are in One Basket

For those of you (you're probably a corporate executive, but this advice applies to anyone in this position) with a large position concentrated in one stock, re-read Chap. 3, "Wealth: How Much Do You Need; How Much Is Enough." Your career has been good to you; the company stock has been flying. You may often ask yourself whether it is too good to be true. There are a handful of company founders who hold their stock through thick and thin—whether it is going up or going down. Warren Buffett is a good example. Control of his company is more important than a known risk-free net worth. For the rest of us, a perfect landing from the vaulting horse of a concentrated position is essential to enjoying a comfortable corporate after-life.

The hero and heroine of Chapter 14 in *Investing Strategies*, Dennis and Judy Jones experienced a "near miss" that could have markedly altered their fortune. For those unfamiliar with their story, Dennis and Judy Jones were high school sweethearts who began their married life living in a small trailer while Dennis was in the Marines at Cherry Point, North Carolina. In 1981, they took their life savings, $100,000, and formed Jones Medical Industries, which later grew into the NASDAQ-listed Jones Pharma (ticker JMED).

In 2000, the Joneses received a buyout offer from King Pharmaceuticals (NYSE: KG) that would yield a market cap of $3.6 billion (inclusive of other employees and public shareholders). Public SEC filings showed that the Jones' pre-tax share of the buyout was worth approximately $400 million in King stock, which was trading at around $40 per share. Sixty days after the transaction closed, SEC handcuff rules prohibiting stock sales by large shareholders expired. King stock, by that time, had rallied to nearly $50 per share, adding another $100 million to their take and another 25% for other shareholders. The post-conversion value of the JMED stock was now $4.2 billion in King stock. Stock analysts that covered King continued to issue buy ratings, and Dennis confided in me that some analysts thought King had the same traits as Jones Pharma in its infancy. If this turned out to be true, the JMED shareholders might experience another ten bagger (meaning they could earn ten times their money if they held onto the stock until their stake was valued at $4 billion).

Nevertheless, on November 6, 2000, the Joneses filed an SEC form 144 indicating the sale of their first $100 million of King stock. Since the entire market, and the specialty pharmaceuticals group, continued to rally, the fact that the Joneses were selling had no impact on the stock. The $55 million the couple donated to a charitable entity was a public transaction viewable in their IRS filed 990 document. Some corporate insiders cringe at the thought of having to publicly disclose that they are selling company stock but Dennis didn't mind; he felt that the public notice was something his 500 employees and other public shareholders were entitled to know. They were free to hold their King stock, but they would know (through the public filings) that he planned to engage in large-scale diversification. By January 1, 2001, people stopped paying attention and the Joneses went about their daily lives.

You know the rest of the story. In 2001, the tech bubble, which had already started to stress, burst, and, combined with the financial panic that accompanied the terrorist attacks of 9/11, the market collapsed. King stock eventually tumbled to an intra-day low of $5 to $7 per share. The 90% drop that King shareholders experienced from its peak to trough mirrored the 90% drop in the Dow Jones Industrial average between 1929 and 1932. King stock recovered a little and the company was purchased by Pfizer for cash at $14 per share on October 12, 2010. Imagine for a second where the Joneses would be if they hadn't decided to step off the train. What if they had decided that what they reaped from the sale of Jones wasn't enough and that they would hold out for more?

Selling the company is a bittersweet proposition for company founders. What appears on paper to be a very lucrative financial outcome is married to the loss of their "baby." Once the company is sold, the former CEO/founders often feel that they have lost their clout in society. The opportunity to have a son, daughter, or grandchild one day running the company vanishes. Having said that, when fatigue catches up with age and the numbers on paper appear to be overly generous, saying yes to the dress becomes easier. If you sell your company, you must be willing to be perfectly happy for the buyer if the stock and company continue to do well without you. You sold it; it's not yours anymore.

I remember when one such CEO declared his wishes and attitude toward future growth in his net worth. After seeing his company stock rally to $50 million, he said, "Enough." He informed the board of his desire to fully retire in two years and said that he would be willing to stay on as chairman, though he would no longer maintain an office at the company headquarters. The board agreed to this arrangement, and the CEO sold stock every quarter when the 144 window was open until he had fully divested himself of the stock (which took approximately three years). Then he did one more unique thing: He declared that he would put 100% of his portfolio into high-grade tax-exempt bonds. (This is the gentleman with the 100% bond portfolio discussed in Chap. 8.) "I have already had my inflation hedge when I owned the company stock. I don't need it anymore. Whether I earn 5% or 2% on my portfolio, I will happily live off interest only and cheer for the guy who replaces me in the corner office."

This man was wealthy, wise, and informed. Some would chide him for going to 100% bonds, but he didn't care. He had enough. When it comes time to decide whether you have enough, have that conversation with yourself and your spouse while walking on the beach or viewing a snow-capped mountain from the front porch of a cabin. If you try to make that decision with your calculator and a copy of *Forbes* on your desk, you might get distracted.

10

Taxation at the Top: Its Long-Term Effect on the Assets

Taxes are as old as civilization. The earliest records date back to at least 3000 BC in ancient Egypt. Citizens would pay biannual levies on their cattle and grain during an event called the "Following of Horus," a royal tour in which the pharaoh appeared before his people for the express purpose of collecting taxes. This practice gave birth during the fourth dynasty (2625 to 2500 BC) to one of the first tax shelters—royal charters of immunity, which were often granted to the priesthood staff and property of Egyptian temples.[1]

Today, Americans who can e-file their tax returns have it easier than their ancient counterparts who had to send caravans of cattle and grain. At the same time, taxes today seem no less capricious and arbitrary than they did back then. This is especially so for wealthy investors who throughout history have been subject to on-again/off-again estate taxes at widely varying rates and top income tax rates that are constantly in flux.

---

[1] David Silverman, "Taxes in Ancient Egypt," *University of Pennsylvania Almanac*, vol. 48, no. 28, April 2, 2002, http://www.upenn.edu/almanac/v48/n28/AncientTaxes.html.

Updated and adapted from Niall Gannon, 2009 [*Investing Strategies for the High Net Worth Investor*], McGraw-Hill Education. Used by permission.

© The Author(s) 2019
N. J. Gannon, *Tailored Wealth Management*,
https://doi.org/10.1007/978-3-319-99780-3_10

The Income Tax: An Historical Perspective

The first income tax in recorded history was levied in the year 10 AD. Emperor Wang Mang of China instituted a tax on the profits of merchants and artisans to finance loans to the needy.[2] Amid widespread famine and outbreaks of pestilence, Wang died in a peasant rebellion in October of 23. Little was heard or seen of the income tax after that until November 24, 1797, when British Prime Minister William Pitt made his famous budget speech pleading for a "general tax on persons possessed of property commensurate as far as practical with their means" to help finance the war against Napoleon.[3]

After much debate and protest and an ever-increasing deficit from the war, what was initially called a triple-assessment tax metamorphosed into a more conventional graduated income tax in Pitt's Act of 1798, which became effective on January 9, 1799. The tax rates at the time ranged from 1 to 10% of income. The tax was repealed in 1801, then brought back in 1803, and vanished again from 1816 through 1842 when it became a permanent part of British life. As Edwin R. A. Seligman notes in his book *The Income Tax: A Study of the History, Theory and Practice of Income Taxation at Home and Abroad*: "In the main, however, all discussion of the tax was silenced in the face of the gigantic struggle against Napoleon.... As the war drew to a close, however, a movement was set on foot to compel the government to redeem its pledge and to drop the tax."[4] That agitation led to its temporary repeal, but in the wake of mounting budget deficits and the failure of customs taxes to foot the bill, the Act of 1842 brought the tax back.

The income tax in the United States followed a similar pattern. What initially began as customs and property taxes in the colonies became an income tax in the wake of the bloody and immensely costly Civil War. While, prior to the war, some states imposed a crude kind of income tax called the *faculty tax* to tax those who didn't own property (property or land was already taxed), mounting war costs prompted Congress to pass the Revenue Act of August 5, 1861, which authorized the country's first federal income tax of 3% on all citizens earning more than $800 a year. The following year the Revenue Act of 1862 created the country's first graduated income tax of 3% on annual incomes above $600 and 5% on those above $10,000. That same year

---

[2] Charles O. Hucker, *China's Imperial Past* (Palo Alto: Stanford University Press, 1995), p. 190.
[3] Edwin R. A. Seligman, *The Income Tax: A Study of the History, Theory and Practice of Income Taxation at Home and Abroad* (New York: The Macmillan Company, 1911), p. 62.
[4] Ibid., p. 106.

Congress created the Bureau of Internal Revenue, a precursor to the Internal Revenue Service (IRS), and Abraham Lincoln appointed its first commissioner, George S. Boutwell, a former governor of Massachusetts.

When Boutwell was sworn in on July 16, 1862, he was given an office on the first floor of the Treasury building and assigned three clerks. By January 1, 1863, his office had grown to employ nearly 4000 people, including 365 tax collectors and property assessors.[5] The subsequent Revenue Act of 1864 raised rates to 5% for people with incomes over $600, 7.5% for incomes between $5000 and $10,000, and 10% for incomes greater than $10,000.[6] Despite the predictable explosion in federal bureaucracy, what modern readers may find remarkable is that the income tax act actually had a sunset clause built into it. Congress allowed it to expire in 1872 as the populace mainly viewed it as an emergency measure for wartime situations. From that point until the ratification of the Constitution's Sixteenth Amendment in 1913 the federal government was supported primarily by excise taxes and tariffs.

The Sixteenth Amendment ushered in the modern income tax era, and I suppose from the high net worth investor's perspective it may seem all downhill from there. But it's important to remember, first, that high excise taxes and tariffs on trade were ultimately very bad for a burgeoning economy, so the income tax provided some necessary relief. Second, paying income taxes at 37% rates in 2019 may seem like a lot, but that's nothing compared to their peak rate of 94% in 1944. As these swings illustrate, it's absolutely crucial for wealthy investors to learn from tax history, keep abreast of tax trends, and factor after-tax returns into their portfolio strategies.

Consider Fig. 10.1 showing the top marginal income tax brackets from 1916 through 2018 and you will see how variable they can be.

As you can see, the lowest US top marginal brackets in the modern tax era were 24% in 1929 and 25% throughout the latter half of the roaring 1920s, a time of major economic growth in the United States. Unfortunately, that growth and the excesses it inspired created a major stock market bubble that ushered in the Great Depression. Rates were also relatively low in the 1990s, another time of accelerating economic growth and technological innovation, which ultimately led to two major stock market crashes, from 2000 through 2002 and in 2008. Some might argue that the low tax rates helped create the economic boom; others may say they were a reaction to it, since the govern-

---

[5] Gary Giroux and Sharon Johns, "Financing the Civil War: the Office of Internal Revenue and the Use of Revenue Stamps," paper presented at the Academy of Accounting Historians International Accounting History Colloquium, 2000, http://acct.tamu.edu/giroux/financingcivil.htm.

[6] Seligman, *The Income Tax*, p. 444.

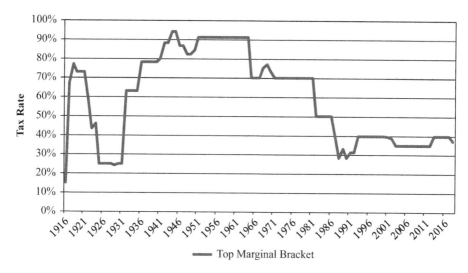

Fig. 10.1 Top marginal tax bracket

ment needs less tax revenue per capita when the economy is soaring and the federal coffers are already full. This debate cannot be resolved easily, but for wealthy investors all that matters is that they position their portfolios accordingly.

The highest top marginal tax brackets, as we've seen throughout history, seem to peak as a result of war or severe economic stress. The first twentieth-century peak of 77% occurred in 1918 in reaction to the United States entering World War I in 1917. After the war ended, the top rates fell back down to 25%.

According to Sheldon David Pollack, author of *The Failure of U.S. Tax Policy: Revenue and Politics*: "America's entry into World War I resulted in an increase in the federal government's demand for revenue that far exceeded all initial estimates. Revenue projections from [the] Treasury were constantly revised upward as estimates by the military of the costs of war invariably proved to be understated. In fact, the cost of the first full year of American participation in the war was $26 billion—more than the total cost of the entire federal government from 1791 through 1917. Such an explosion in federal expenditures could hardly have failed to occasion a fiscal revolution. As had been the case during the 1860s, the revenue crisis fueled by war led to fundamental changes in the structure of the federal income tax."[7]

---

[7] Sheldon David Pollack, *The Failure of U.S. Tax Policy: Revenue and Politics* (University Park, PA: Penn State Press, 1999), p. 55.

The second major twentieth-century increase in income taxes occurred in 1932 as the country was neck deep in the Great Depression, and President Franklin Roosevelt's New Deal caused federal expenditures to expand. Top federal tax rates rose from 25% in 1931 to 63% in 1932 and then to 78% by 1936. The Social Security Act of 1935 created not only retirement benefits, but also unemployment benefits and welfare benefits for the poor and handicapped. That of course caused expenditures to grow significantly.

During World War II income taxes peaked at 94% in 1944. Top rates subsequently hovered around 90% until 1965 when they dropped to 70% because of President Lyndon Johnson's Revenue Act of 1964, and then to 50% in 1982 as a result of President Ronald Reagan's Economic Recovery Tax Act of 1981 and, with the 1986 Tax Reform Act, they dropped to 28% during his presidency. Unfortunately, as a consequence of these tax cuts and a large increase in military spending, the federal deficit grew significantly during Reagan's tenure. To those who knew tax history, it seemed inevitable that taxes would bounce back up, and they did to 33% during George H. W. Bush's presidency and then to 39.6% under Bill Clinton.

Congress, under President Obama, passed a one-year extension of the Bush rates and then raised the rate back to 39.6% in 2013. In addition to an increase in the top marginal rate in 2013, a Medicare surtax of 3.8% on net investment income was imposed as part of the Affordable Health Care Act. This created an effective top marginal bracket of 43.4% for investors and a combined federal and state income tax rate exceeding 55% for investors residing in California or New York.

The Tax Cuts and Jobs Act of 2017 (which became effective in 2018), signed by President Trump, dropped the top marginal tax rate to 37% (or 40.8% effective rate for those who pay the Medicare surtax on investment income). While at first glance this appeared to provide minor tax relief at the top bracket, it did not because the legislation also removed the ability to deduct state and local taxes along with miscellaneous other deductions from the federal return. As a result, the Trump tax legislation ranged from being a non-event for taxpayers in low- or no state income tax states such as Florida to a significant tax increase for taxpayers in high state taxes like California or New York. The loss of the deductibility of state and local taxes cost these taxpayers more than the reduction of the top marginal bracket saved for them.

As 2018 brought more clarity as to the impact of the new law, tax advisors counseled investors to look at the big picture, that is, their total taxation situation. For investors who experienced a tax increase due to the loss of the deductibility of state and local taxes, the reduction in the corporate income tax rate from 35 to 21% left companies with more net income in the cash register, which they could use to pay dividends, make capital expenditures, hire additional workers, or reduce debt.

Adjusting Your Portfolio to Suit the Income Tax Times

Although little can be done about the taxation of employment income (except to move to low tax states; see Chap. 11) for wealthy business owners and executives, there's no reason they should have to suffer high taxation on their portfolio assets as investors. As the above history reveals, income tax rates can be incredibly volatile and unpredictable. But whatever the prevailing rates are at the time, investors should do the math and calculate what the after-tax return on their investments will be and invest accordingly.

Note: When optimizing their portfolios, investors should be aware that there are some investment strategies and asset classes that are more affected by income taxes than others. In general, low-turnover equity strategies, long-term private equity, and municipal bonds are considered tax efficient. High-turnover equity, corporate bonds, US government bonds, hedge funds, commodity trading, and bank certificates of deposits are considered tax inefficient.

Stock dividends are an interesting case, as sometimes they have been taxed as income and sometimes they haven't. From 1913 through 1935 dividends were completely tax exempt, whereas from 1936 through 1939 they were fully taxable as income, only to be exempted again through 1953. From 1953 through 2002, they were again taxed as income, but the IRS allowed minor exemptions of up to $100. With the Jobs and Growth Tax Reconciliation Act of 2003 dividends were taxed at the 15% rate. Although the preferential rate on dividends was expected to be retired at the end of 2010, it was extended through the end of 2012. Beginning in 2013, the dividend and capital gains tax rose to 20%, while still subjecting investors to the 3.8% Medicare net investment income tax.

Although the tax-free status of municipal bonds seems relatively secure, even they haven't been completely immune from controversy. According to a 1988 ruling by the US Supreme Court on a case titled *South Carolina v. Baker*, there is no constitutional guarantee of municipal bonds being exempt from federal taxes, and Congress could pass legislation to tax the bonds if it wanted to.[8]

---

[8] Mark T. Green and Fred Thompson, *Handbook of Public Finance* (Boca Raton: CRC Press, 1998), p. 487.

Given the historical instability of tax rates, the question will ultimately crop up when designing a portfolio as to where they are heading in future years. Obviously, there is a degree of unpredictability to the answer. But if history is any guide, during times of war, economic stress, and large budget deficits, income tax rates on the wealthy tend to go up. So it should come as no surprise to wealthy investors when tax rates increase during prolonged economic downturns.

An increase in taxes forces investors to adjust their net portfolio return expectations. It leads us to a fork in the road where we must decide whether we are going to allocate our portfolio assets based upon the returns that we desire or based upon the returns that are possible, which leads to a divergence between two groups. Some acknowledge those lower rates of return in traditional asset classes, but still try ever so hard to capture 10 to 11% compounding. The only mathematical way to do that (since it is difficult to get that return in equities or in bonds) is to speculate on hedge funds, private equity, and commodities. Those who choose this route should consider this startling fact: should taxes rise to the level of those during the Carter administration (1977–1980), a commodity or hedge fund would need to produce a gross return of 33.75% in order to produce a 6% return to investors net of all taxes and fees. This is because during that period, fund returns were taxed at the then top marginal bracket of 70% and they would also have been subject to the 2%/20% fee structure of the hedge fund.

The other group is going to say that I'm unwilling to gamble everything that I have accumulated and amassed in my business by betting on the price of agricultural goods or metals, and I'm going to adjust either my spending rates or my multigenerational view of how these assets will affect my family. This group, I think, will have a more realistic understanding of what's possible in this environment.

Adjusting Your Portfolio to Suit the Capital Gains Tax Times

Generally speaking, through much of US history long-term capital gains tax rates have been lower than income tax rates. The reason for this is the belief that capital investment spurs economic growth and shouldn't be penalized with onerous taxes. And yet rates have crept up significantly from time to time. If you review Fig. 10.2, you can see how they've changed since 1916.

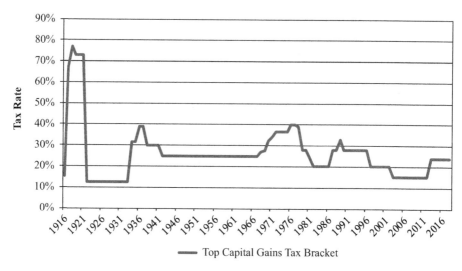

Fig. 10.2   Top capital gains tax bracket

As you can see, initially capital gains tax rates mirrored those of income taxes because such gains were originally treated the same as income under the Sixteenth Amendment. As a result, in 1918 the top capital gains tax rate was a shocking 77%. As you might expect, investors soon complained that such high rates were an impediment to the flow of capital. According to Jeremy Siegel, author of *Stocks for the Long Run*: "Until 1921 there was no tax preference given to capital gains income. When tax rates were increased sharply during World War I, investors refrained from realizing gains and complained to Congress about the tax consequences of selling their assets. Congress was persuaded that such 'frozen portfolios' were detrimental to the efficient allocation of capital, and so in 1922 a maximum tax rate of 12.5% was established on capital gains income."[9]

Subsequent to 1922, maximum capital gains tax rates were always lower than maximum income tax rates, except in 1989 when both were capped at 33% in an attempt to simplify things. The lower rates are meant to encourage people to invest in the capital markets and have been generally structured to encourage long-term investment. Sometimes the rates have been complicated by various "exclusions." This policy meant capital gains were still considered income, but a portion of the gain was completely excluded from taxation. According to Leonard Burman and Deborah Kobes of the Tax Policy Center:

---

[9] Jeremy Siegel, *Stocks for the Long Run: The Definitive Guide to Financial Market Returns and Long-Term Investment Strategies* (New York: McGraw Hill, 2007), p. 74.

"Since 1934, capital gains tax preferences have generally been affected by means of an exclusion—that is, a portion of long-term capital gains were excluded from tax. For example, from 1982 to 1986, 60% of long-term capital gains were excluded from being taxed. Since the top tax rate on ordinary income was 50%, this implies a top effective tax rate on capital gains of 20%."[10] That 20% effective rate is derived by taking half of the remaining 40% of capital gains taxed as income after factoring in the exclusion.

The use of the exclusion led to some interesting benefits for the long-term investor. For instance, in 1934 and 1935, 20, 40, 60, and 70% of gains were excluded on assets held one, two, five, and ten years, respectively; investors who held equities for less than one year received no exclusion. Since the maximum income tax rate at the time was 63%, the effective maximum capital gains tax rate for the truly long-term investor, those who held on for ten years and sold in 1934, would have been just 18.9%—that is, 63% of the 30% remaining of the capital gain that was taxable as income. Meanwhile, the investor who held his stocks for less than one year would be taxed at a maximum rate of 63%. If such a taxation system were instituted today, the differences in after-tax returns between low-turnover and high-turnover strategies would be extreme.

Although long-term capital gains rates have generally been lower than income tax rates, it is always important to pay attention to the difference between the two because it can affect your portfolio strategy. For instance, in 1922 and 1989 when income and capital gains tax rates were the same, there was no apparent tax benefit (assuming equal return potential) to owning stocks over taxable bonds such as Treasuries because they were taxed identically. There was also no tax benefit to being a long-term investor. But the wider the gap between income tax rates and capital gains tax rates, the greater the advantage tax-wise long-term stock investors have. In a year like 1944, when income tax rates were as high as 94% while capital gains taxes were only 25%, stocks would have a distinct advantage over taxable bonds.

Of course, one unique advantage non-dividend-paying stocks always have over taxable bonds, regardless of the tax rate, is the control they give to investors. If you invest in stocks that appreciate, you can wait to sell the stock and realize the gain until capital gains tax rates are lower. If you invest in taxable bonds, you have no choice but to pay the taxes on the bonds as the income is paid. The timing of a stock sale can have a huge significance to wealthy investors

---

[10] Leonard E. Burman and Deborah Kobes, "Preferential Capital Gains Tax Rates," *Tax Notes*, January 19, 2004, p. 411, http://www.taxpolicycenter.org/publications/url.cfm?ID=1000588.

whose net worth is tied up in shares of public or private businesses they founded or run. For them, it is absolutely essential to pay attention to what the current capital gains tax rates are when they think about selling and to calculate what the comparable after-tax returns will be for other investments they are thinking of purchasing with the proceeds of their sale. This is especially true for a family that is considering a sale of its business.

The prevailing capital gains tax rate will have a large impact on how a stock investment compares to a tax-free municipal bond investment. The higher the capital gains rate is, the less attractive stocks look compared to bonds after taxes. That said, in my own experience as an investor, portfolio strategy should not be trumped by tax strategy unless the fundamentals dictate otherwise. Consider the example of a CEO of a Nasdaq-listed technology company who received an offer to sell the company in 2000. She may have been convinced that long-term capital gains rates were headed lower and that delaying the sale until that time would save money on taxes. Though she would have been correct about this, waiting would have saved her 5% in taxes; delaying the sale likely exposed her to 50% or more in losses (as valuation levels in the market dropped between 2000 and 2003). Clearly, this investor would have been better off economically paying the higher capital gains tax than the waiting.

When the rate on capital gains taxation increased in 2013 from 15 to 23.8% (inclusive of the 3.8% Medicare net investment income tax), it represented a 59% increase in the dollar amount paid on a year-over-year comparison of 2013 versus 2012. Remember, a low-turnover equity strategy (20% turnover or less) means that even if the rate remains static, it is levied only on realized capital gains. Long-term investors who manage to successfully hold businesses over time will at least delay the payment of embedded unrealized taxes on long-term capital gains.

Adjusting Your Portfolio to Suit the Estate Tax Times

The modern estate tax in the United States can trace its roots back to 1906 and President Theodore Roosevelt, who felt that robber barons such as Andrew Carnegie and John D. Rockefeller wielded too much power and that allowing them to pass their massive estates down from one generation to the next in perpetuity posed a threat to US democracy. Although some form of "death tax" existed in ancient times and in the United States prior to 1916, mostly such taxes were considered temporary measures to raise revenue during wartime.

But it was Roosevelt who in his famous 1906 State of the Union address and "The Man with the Muck-rake" speeches pushed for the progressive reforms that led to the Sixteenth Amendment in 1913 and the Revenue Act of 1916.

Politics aside, the ostensible impetus for the estate tax part of the Revenue Act of 1916 was to pay for America's involvement in World War I. The initial tax was just 1% on estates over $50,000 and 10% for amounts over $5 million. As you can see from Fig. 10.3, the maximum rate has changed dramatically over time.

Throughout history there have always been various exemptions and exclusions that allowed families to protect a certain portion of their estates from taxes. According to a history of the estate tax compiled by John Luckey of the Congressional Research Service, "The 1916 estate tax allowed the executor to reduce a decedent's estate for tax purposes by a $50,000 exemption and the amount of any funeral expenses, administration expenses, debts, losses, and claims against the estate."[11] But while such exemptions and exclusions grew over time, so did the top tax rate on the wealthiest estates.

In many respects, the rates followed a pattern similar to that of income taxes. So while estate tax rates rose during World War I from 10 to 25%, in

Fig. 10.3   Estate tax rates

---

[11] John R. Luckey, "A History of Federal Estate, Gift, and Generation-Skipping Taxes," Congressional Research Service, April 9, 2003, p. CRS-7.

the early 1920s, the anger over high taxes after the war ended and the unbri-dled enthusiasm of the Roaring Twenties inspired Congress to cut the rate to 20% and to double the estate exemption to $100,000 in 1926. But as with income taxes, estate tax rates soared during the Great Depression from 20 to 45% in 1932 and then to 70% from 1935 to 1940, peaking finally at 77% from 1941 through 1976. And then, like income taxes, they declined again.

One of the unique quirks of the estate tax code resulted from the passage of President George W. Bush's Economic Growth and Tax Relief Reconciliation Act of 2001, which led to no estate tax in 2010; thereafter it bounced back to 55%. Some advisors at the time joked that wealthy parents shouldn't leave their drinks unattended around their children at their 2010 Christmas party. The 2017 Trump tax reform plan reduced the top estate tax rate to 40% beginning on January 1, 2018.

What is also interesting is how dramatically the dollar amount to be taxed at the maximum estate tax rate has changed over time. If you review Fig. 10.4, you will see that the dollar amounts by no means follow in lockstep with the rates themselves.

So, for instance, while estate tax rates went up in 1917 from 10 to 25%, the dollar amount to be taxed at that rate also rose from $5 million to $10 mil-lion, a curious fact in a country with a government hungry for revenue during wartime. It stayed at $10 million through the 1920s, but the desire to tax only the superrich at the highest rate grew even stronger during the Depression-era 1930s. According to Luckey of the Congressional Research Service: "Between

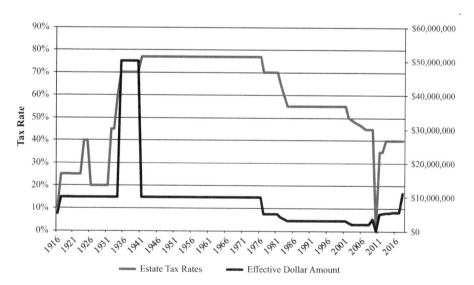

Fig. 10.4 Historical estate tax rates versus dollar amounts

1934 and 1942, social policies and wartime demands led to a series of estate and gift tax rate increases, though the gift tax rates continued to be maintained at three-quarters of the estate tax rates. The Revenue Act of 1934 raised the maximum estate tax rate to 60%, on a net estate over $10,000,000, and the Revenue Act of 1935 further raised it to 70% on net estates over $50,000,000."[12]

After 1940, the government started applying the maximum estate tax rate on increasingly smaller dollar amounts—an alarming trend given that in inflation-adjusted terms a million dollars was actually worth a lot less in the decades after 1940. So 1940 70% tax on estates over $50 million became a 77% tax on estates worth $10 million in 1941. Rates and dollar amounts remained there through 1976. Then in 1977 the rate became 70% for estates over $5 million; at the same time, the dollar amount for the maximum tax rate continued to shrink. Meanwhile, the exclusions and exemptions started to rise so that the estate tax began to apply to a narrower range of wealthy people. For instance, in 1976, anyone with an estate worth more than $60,000 was subject to a minimum estate tax of 3%, while those with over $10 million were subject to the maximum 77% rate. By 2007, only people with a minimum estate value of $2 million were subject to the minimum estate tax of 18%, while anyone with an estate worth more than $3 million was subject to the maximum estate tax rate of 45%.

Inflation and the decreasing dollar amount required to be subject to estate taxes can have a serious impact on small businesses and family farms. Although in Depression-era America a family farmer or small business having a net worth of more than $3 million was relatively uncommon, by the year 2000 when estate taxes were 55% for estates that size, there were a number of occurrences in which, in order to pay the estate tax, the family business or farm needed to be sold, sometimes at distressed prices to vulture investors, because the family didn't have the liquid cash to pay the tax.

For this reason alone wealthy families should have ironclad estate plans long before the founding generation of a business passes away. Liquidating a business in retirement to build a diversified portfolio not only protects the family's assets but should also provide the necessary cash to pay the estate taxes when the business's founder dies. Illiquid assets pose a unique threat to heirs because they lose the ability to time the sale of assets for payment of estate taxes. A decedent, who died in March 2008, with a high allocation to an illiquid private business, real estate, or hedge fund may have lost his entire estate because of that year's recession.

---

[12] Ibid., p. CRS-9.

If the decedent's portfolio had a market value of $100 million on the date of his death, March 31, 2008, the 45% effective estate tax would result in a tax of $45 million. If he were a resident of the state of New Jersey, he might be subject to up to an additional 16% of the gross estate[13] or $16 million. If the value of the estate fell in line with the broad stock market averages (−48.9%),[14] the value of the combined federal and state estate tax bill would exceed the value of the entire portfolio.

Though the above are examples of a rare "perfect storm," wealthy investors should consider the mathematical effects of such events.

The 2017 tax reform signed by President Trump included a large increase in the estate tax exemption for tax years beginning in 2018 and going through 2025. It allows an individual to receive an exemption of $11.2 million and $22.4 million for a married couple. This provision provides relatively trivial estate tax relief for multibillionaires, but it did satisfy a more universal appeal that it protected family farmers and small business owners. Note: These families should not assume that the exemption will hold past the year 2025 as it will expire without congressional action.

One family I work with had 99% of its portfolio invested in its company stock from 1981 to 1996. It experienced six 50% corrections resulting from declines in the value of its company stock in the 1980s and 1990s. Near the end of the 1990s, it sold the company and invested the entire proceeds of the sale in our balanced portfolio. This was fortunate, because in the subsequent bear market of 2001 to 2002, the company stock declined by 75%. The two bear markets of 2001 to 2002 and 2008 to 2009 had muted effects on the family's total portfolio because of the presence of bonds, a reduced equity exposure, and the absence of alternative investments. In the case of this family, had the owner of the company stock chosen to continue to hold the bulk of the portfolio in the concentrated holding and died any time between July of 2001 and April of 2004, the estate tax bill would have completely wiped out any residual value for the heirs. Because the stock was publicly traded, the family would have had a difficult time arguing for a discount on the actual value of the estate on the date of death.

In later chapters, we will discuss gifting strategies during the founder's life, which are generally a more efficient means of transferring assets to one's heirs.

---

[13] Fein, Such, Kahn, and Shepard, "New Tax Laws: Separate New Jersey Estate Tax," 2002.
[14] Baseline (Thomson Financial) value of S&P 500 index on March 31, 2008:1322.7, value on March 9, 2009: 676.53.

Adjusting Your Portfolio to Suit the Gift Tax Times

The origin of the gift tax really goes hand in hand with the estate tax. Luckey puts it best, "The gift tax has developed as a necessary concomitant to the death tax because the easiest way to escape a tax on the gratuitous transfer of property at death is to divest oneself of the property during life. The impact of either tax alone would be diminished by the escape offered by the alternate transfer."[15] The tax was first introduced in the Revenue Act of 1924 to close the loopholes in the original 1916 estate tax law, then repealed by the Revenue Act of 1926—during that by now familiar Roaring Twenties period of anti-tax activism—and then reintroduced permanently by the Revenue Act of 1932 during the Depression.

As you can see from Fig. 10.5, gift tax rates have been as capricious and all over the map as the estate tax.

And yet one of the key advantages of the gift tax historically has often been that it is lower than the estate tax. Up until 1977 the gift tax rate was generally

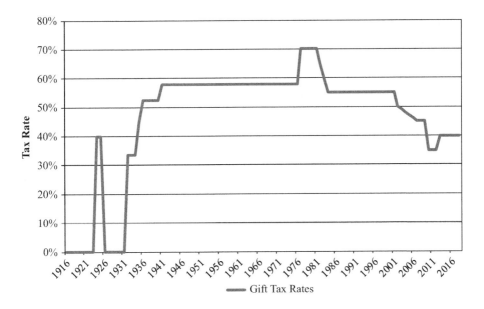

Fig. 10.5 Gift tax rates

---

[15] Luckey, "A History of Federal Estate, Gift, and Generation-Skipping Taxes," p. CRS-1.

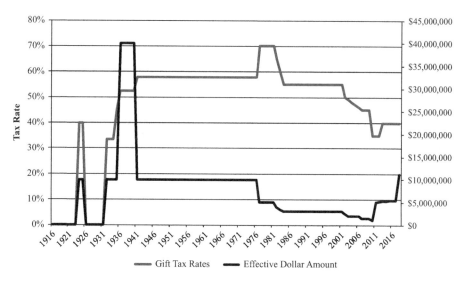

Fig. 10.6 Historical gift tax rates versus dollar amounts

about three-fourths of the prevailing estate tax rate. With such a discount it made sense to give your heirs their inheritance during your lifetime. But, as we shall see from real-life case studies, even when gift tax rates matched estate tax rates as they have in recent years, it still generally makes more sense for wealthy investors to gift because of the potential for greater capital appreciation and the way gift taxes are calculated; the gift tax is assessed on the net amount received by the heirs whereas the estate tax is assessed on the gross amount of the estate.

As you can tell from Fig. 10.6, the dollar amounts subject to the maximum gift tax rate have generally mirrored that of the estate tax. But it's important to note that the lifetime unified tax credit on the gift tax differs from the annual gift tax exclusion. In 2010, for instance, wealthy investors could gift $13,000 per year to each of their heirs, and this in no way reduced the $1 million lifetime gift tax exclusion. The 2017 tax reform, which became effective in 2018, raised the annual gift tax exclusion to $14,000. It should be noted that a married couple can effectively gift $56,000 without tax to another married couple because the law allows each member of the gifting couple to make a $14,000 gift to each member of the receiving couple.

Perhaps the most significant reform to both estate and gift taxes occurred in the Tax Reform Act of 1976. According to an estate tax history compiled by the IRS's Statistics of Income Division: "This act created a unified estate and gift tax framework that consisted of a 'single, graduated rate of tax imposed on both lifetime gifts and testamentary dispositions.' Prior to the act, 'it cost substantially more to leave property at death than to give it away during life,' due to the lower tax rate applied to gifts. The Tax Reform Act of 1976 also merged the estate tax exclusion and the lifetime gift tax exclusion into a 'single, unified estate and gift tax credit, which may be used to offset gift tax liability during the donor's lifetime but which, if unused at death, is available to offset the deceased donor's estate tax liability.'"[16]

The 1976 act also introduced a tax on generation-skipping trusts, thus closing a loophole whereby the children of the estate's founding family benefited from the income produced by the estate without paying estate taxes because the parents put the assets in a trust for the grandchildren, thereby "skipping" the generation to be subject to the estate tax. It is notable that the 2017 tax reform passed by Congress also increased the generation-skipping tax exclusion to $11.2 million per individual to match the estate tax exclusion amount. As the existence of the estate tax proves in more ways than one, there are two things you can't escape in life—death and taxes.

Conclusions

- Taxes are an inescapable part of history.
- Income tax rates tend to go up during times of war and economic crisis.
- The wider the gap between income and capital gains tax rates, the more attractive stocks become when compared to taxable bonds.
- Investors in stocks shouldn't let taxes alone dictate their decision to sell.
- Families that don't plan for estate taxes can lose their businesses.
- Gifting generally carries less of a tax burden than estate taxes.

With this in mind, whether you own your own business, have your money invested in stocks or bonds or your company's stock, it is important to recognize and plan for the impact of taxes on your investment decisions.

---

[16] Darien B. Jacobson, Brian G. Raub, and Barry W. Johnson, "The Estate Tax: Ninety Years and Counting," *SOI Bulletin*, Summer 2007, p. 122, http://www.irs.gov/pub/irs-soi/ninetyestate.pdf.

11

Portfolio Optimization: The Impact of Taxation, Turnover, and Time Horizon on Net Returns

In a sense, I added "researcher" to my résumé in the summer of 2005 when I attended the Wharton/IPI Private Wealth Management Program, a one-week program held twice a year at the Wharton Executive Education Center. During that week I suddenly realized that there was a gaping hole in the study of equity and asset allocation research: nobody had completed a study to determine the after-tax return on equity portfolios taxed at the top bracket.

Encouraged by Charlotte Beyer and intellectually stimulated by Professor Dick Marston, the founders of the program, I resolved to construct an unabridged model of the S&P 500 Index back to its founding in 1957 to determine what happened to the portfolios of those taxed at the then-prevailing top bracket in each of those years. The model also took into account the impact of state taxation. There had been, up to that point, attempts to study net returns but those studies did not specifically observe the impact on top bracket taxation; they omitted state taxation; and/or they did not examine post-liquidation results. Jean Brunel, editor of the *Journal of Wealth Management*, agreed to publish the resulting paper which was co-authored by Michael Blum. Since 2013, the model has been updated and refined by Scott B. Seibert, CFA. Scott's work over the past five years has been instrumental not only in our after-tax research but in the formulation and publication of the Efficient Valuation Hypothesis revised paper.

The main objective of the paper was not only to calculate the after-tax return on equities, but also to compare stock and bond returns on a net basis. Thus, we were trying to observe the after-tax equity risk premium (or lack of risk premium) that was available to investors throughout the period. We supposed (when we began the study) that there were times when bonds outperformed equities on a net basis. That supposition turned out to be

© The Author(s) 2019
N. J. Gannon, *Tailored Wealth Management*,
https://doi.org/10.1007/978-3-319-99780-3_11

correct. When examining rolling 20-year periods beginning in 1957, we found that municipal bond portfolios outperformed equity portfolios 17% of the time. Just as important, we realized that this forward-looking outperformance could be observed *at the beginning of the period* in half of those instances.

Without the 2006 study and subsequent updates over the following decade, the Efficient Valuation Hypothesis (discussed in Chap. 7) might not have come into being. We believed then, and we staunchly believe now, that the notion that stocks outperform fixed income over time (popularly referred to as stocks for the long run[1]) is false when examining net returns over specific periods. We proved in that paper that the equity risk premium (the excess return earned in a stock portfolio versus a bond portfolio) in the highest bracket is greatly diminished (or even negative at specific times) compared with a non-taxable portfolio such as an endowment or a qualified retirement account, which together provide the baseline used by most investors when making investment decisions. Thus, if an IRA investor invests in the S&P and earns 10%, a taxable investor would receive 7%, which is why high net worth investors need a more customized approach when making investment decisions.

When you review the tables in this chapter, you may find yourself over-emphasizing the averages that were observed over the entire length of the study. To avoid this, I recommend that you train your eyes on the shorter 20-year period to see how remarkably different the returns actually were.

To summarize:

- The price (P/E ratio) one pays for a business or a group of businesses matters.
- The tax rate, inclusive of taxes on dividends, long-term capital gains, and state taxes, matters.
- The interest rate available on a 20-year non-taxable municipal bond in the investor's home state matters.

Effect of a High Tax Bracket on After-Tax Returns on Stocks 1957 to 2017

We chose to begin our study of after-tax equity risk premium with 1957 because that is when the Standard & Poor's 500 Index was first published.[2] We ended our study with December 31, 2017. Table 11.1 illustrates a

---

[1] The term "stocks for the long run" was coined by Jeremy J. Siegel and is the title of his book *Stocks for the Long Run: The Definitive Guide to Financial Market Returns & Long-Term Investment Strategies*, which was originally published in 1994 and is currently in its fifth edition, McGraw-Hill Education, 2014.

[2] Standard & Poor's Web site www.standardandpoors.com contains the history of the Index, which dates to 1923. It was expanded to include 500 companies in 1957.

Table 11.1 S&P 500 taxed at top income bracket

Year	S&P beg price	S&P end price	S&P return	Div yield	Div amount	Div after tax	Ord income tax %	LT cap gains tax	LT cap gains tax on realized gain	Embedded capital gains	Beg cost basis	End cost basis	Beg portfolio	End portfolio
1957	44.72	41.12	−8.05%	1.75%	$1.66	$0.05	91.00%	25.00%	$0.00	$0.00	$100.00	$99.65	$100.00	$92.00
1958	41.12	55.62	35.26%	1.83%	$2.05	$0.06	91.00%	25.00%	$0.38	$23.55	$99.65	$100.56	$92.00	$124.12
1959	55.62	58.03	4.33%	1.95%	$2.49	$0.07	91.00%	25.00%	$0.45	$27.48	$100.56	$101.64	$124.12	$129.12
1960	58.03	58.11	0.14%	3.41%	$4.41	$0.13	91.00%	25.00%	$0.43	$26.28	$101.64	$102.72	$129.12	$129.00
1961	58.11	71.55	23.13%	2.85%	$4.21	$0.13	91.00%	25.00%	$0.87	$53.31	$102.72	$104.79	$129.00	$158.10
1962	71.55	63.10	−11.81%	3.40%	$4.98	$0.15	91.00%	25.00%	$0.54	$32.91	$104.79	$106.13	$158.10	$139.04
1963	63.10	75.02	18.89%	3.13%	$4.87	$0.15	91.00%	25.00%	$0.92	$56.21	$106.13	$108.32	$139.04	$164.53
1964	75.02	84.75	12.97%	3.05%	$5.42	$0.16	91.00%	25.00%	$1.20	$73.67	$108.32	$111.16	$164.53	$184.83
1965	84.75	92.43	9.06%	3.06%	$5.98	$0.18	91.00%	25.00%	$1.40	$85.90	$111.16	$114.45	$184.83	$200.35
1966	92.43	80.33	−13.09%	3.59%	$6.60	$1.59	70.00%	25.00%	$0.92	$56.69	$114.45	$118.10	$200.35	$174.79
1967	80.33	96.47	20.09%	3.09%	$6.08	$1.46	70.00%	25.00%	$1.42	$87.21	$118.10	$122.72	$174.79	$209.94
1968	96.47	103.86	7.66%	2.93%	$6.45	$1.55	70.00%	25.00%	$1.60	$98.13	$122.72	$127.83	$209.94	$225.96
1969	103.86	92.06	−11.36%	3.52%	$7.39	$1.40	75.00%	26.90%	$1.19	$68.84	$127.83	$131.67	$225.96	$200.51
1970	92.06	92.15	0.10%	3.46%	$6.94	$1.18	77.00%	27.50%	$1.16	$65.59	$131.67	$135.15	$200.51	$200.73
1971	92.15	102.09	10.79%	3.10%	$6.64	$1.59	70.00%	32.30%	$1.67	$82.88	$135.15	$139.43	$200.73	$222.31
1972	102.09	118.05	15.63%	2.70%	$6.59	$1.58	70.00%	34.30%	$2.37	$111.75	$139.43	$144.52	$222.31	$256.27
1973	118.05	97.55	−17.36%	3.70%	$8.45	$2.03	70.00%	36.50%	$1.43	$63.88	$144.52	$148.49	$256.27	$212.37
1974	97.55	68.56	−29.72%	5.43%	$9.39	$2.25	70.00%	36.50%	$0.02	$0.73	$148.49	$150.76	$212.37	$151.50
1975	68.56	90.19	31.55%	4.14%	$7.51	$1.80	70.00%	36.50%	$1.03	$46.10	$150.76	$153.96	$151.50	$200.06
1976	90.19	107.46	19.15%	3.93%	$8.80	$2.11	70.00%	36.50%	$1.79	$80.19	$153.96	$158.50	$200.06	$238.69
1977	107.46	95.10	−11.51%	5.11%	$11.32	$2.72	70.00%	39.90%	$1.21	$50.09	$158.50	$162.64	$238.69	$212.73
1978	95.10	96.11	1.07%	5.39%	$11.54	$2.77	70.00%	39.90%	$1.20	$49.74	$162.64	$166.83	$212.73	$216.57
1979	96.11	107.94	12.31%	5.53%	$12.90	$3.10	70.00%	39.00%	$1.72	$72.58	$166.83	$172.02	$216.57	$244.60
1980	107.94	135.76	25.77%	4.74%	$13.46	$3.23	70.00%	28.00%	$2.31	$128.84	$172.02	$179.73	$244.60	$308.57
1981	135.76	122.55	−9.73%	5.57%	$16.14	$3.87	70.00%	28.00%	$1.68	$93.88	$179.73	$186.87	$308.57	$280.74

(continued)

Table 11.1 (continued)

Year	S&P beg price	S&P end price	S&P return	Div yield	Div amount	Div after tax	Ord income tax %	LT cap gains tax	LT cap gains tax on realized gain	Embedded capital gains	Beg cost basis	End cost basis	Beg portfolio	End portfolio	$100.00
1982	122.55	140.64	14.76%	4.93%	$15.12	$3.63	70.00%	23.70%	$2.01	$128.55	$186.87	$195.25	$280.74	$323.80	$323.80
1983	140.64	164.93	17.27%	4.32%	$15.50	$6.82	50.00%	20.00%	$2.40	$175.25	$195.25	$208.90	$323.80	$384.15	$384.15
1984	164.93	167.24	1.40%	4.68%	$18.14	$7.98	50.00%	20.00%	$2.35	$171.60	$208.90	$223.56	$384.15	$395.16	$395.16
1985	167.24	211.28	26.33%	3.88%	$17.86	$7.86	50.00%	20.00%	$3.58	$261.87	$223.56	$241.61	$395.16	$503.49	$503.49
1986	211.28	242.17	14.62%	3.38%	$18.57	$8.17	50.00%	20.00%	$4.36	$318.71	$241.61	$262.20	$503.49	$580.91	$580.91
1987	242.17	247.08	2.03%	3.71%	$21.82	$9.60	50.00%	20.00%	$4.30	$313.97	$262.20	$284.03	$580.91	$598.00	$598.00
1988	247.08	277.72	12.40%	3.68%	$23.71	$13.16	38.50%	28.00%	$6.60	$368.72	$284.03	$310.00	$598.00	$678.72	$678.72
1989	277.72	353.40	27.25%	3.32%	$26.37	$17.40	28.00%	28.00%	$9.41	$525.99	$310.00	$345.67	$678.72	$871.66	$871.66
1990	353.40	330.22	-6.56%	3.74%	$31.26	$20.63	28.00%	28.00%	$7.97	$445.37	$345.67	$381.78	$871.66	$827.15	$827.15
1991	330.22	417.09	26.31%	3.11%	$29.95	$19.77	28.00%	28.00%	$11.27	$629.82	$381.78	$423.43	$827.15	$1053.25	$1053.25
1992	417.09	435.71	4.46%	2.90%	$31.40	$20.72	28.00%	28.00%	$11.51	$643.00	$423.43	$466.48	$1053.25	$1109.48	$1109.48
1993	435.71	466.45	7.06%	2.72%	$31.51	$19.85	31.00%	28.00%	$12.26	$685.21	$466.48	$510.14	$1109.48	$1195.35	$1195.35
1994	466.45	459.27	-1.54%	2.91%	$34.45	$18.74	39.60%	28.00%	$11.34	$633.47	$510.14	$550.88	$1195.35	$1184.35	$1184.35
1995	459.27	615.93	34.11%	2.30%	$33.05	$17.98	39.60%	28.00%	$18.26	$985.59	$550.88	$602.47	$1184.35	$1588.06	$1588.06
1996	615.93	740.74	20.26%	2.01%	$35.96	$19.56	39.60%	29.20%	$23.01	$1242.02	$602.47	$664.40	$1588.06	$1906.41	$1906.41
1997	740.74	970.43	31.01%	1.60%	$36.41	$19.81	39.60%	29.20%	$32.26	$1741.50	$664.40	$743.60	$1906.41	$2485.10	$2485.10
1998	970.43	1229.23	26.67%	1.32%	$38.27	$20.82	39.60%	29.20%	$31.26	$2284.03	$743.60	$853.38	$2485.10	$3137.41	$3137.41
1999	1229.23	1469.25	19.53%	1.14%	$40.13	$21.83	39.60%	20.00%	$37.66	$2751.81	$853.38	$982.38	$3137.41	$3734.20	$3734.20
2000	1469.25	1320.28	-10.14%	1.23%	$43.02	$23.40	39.60%	20.00%	$30.85	$2254.54	$982.38	$1093.60	$3734.20	$3348.13	$3348.13
2001	1320.28	1148.09	-13.04%	1.37%	$42.13	$22.92	39.60%	20.00%	$23.63	$1726.98	$1093.60	$1183.78	$3348.13	$2910.76	$2910.76
2002	1148.09	879.82	-23.37%	1.83%	$45.49	$24.75	39.60%	20.00%	$13.61	$994.49	$1183.78	$1247.25	$2910.76	$2241.75	$2241.75
2003	879.82	1111.91	26.38%	1.61%	$42.04	$22.87	39.60%	20.00%	$20.62	$1506.56	$1247.25	$1328.80	$2241.75	$2835.36	$2835.36
2004	1111.91	1211.92	8.99%	1.60%	$47.92	$37.85	15.00%	15.00%	$18.50	$1673.50	$1328.80	$1436.24	$2835.36	$3109.74	$3109.74
2005	1211.92	1248.29	3.00%	1.79%	$56.71	$44.80	15.00%	15.00%	$18.55	$1678.48	$1436.24	$1550.83	$3109.74	$3229.31	$3229.31
2006	1248.29	1418.30	13.62%	1.77%	$62.02	$49.00	15.00%	15.00%	$22.24	$2012.38	$1550.83	$1683.50	$3229.31	$3695.88	$3695.88
2007	1418.30	1468.36	3.53%	1.89%	$71.39	$56.40	15.00%	15.00%	$22.50	$2035.69	$1683.50	$1824.54	$3695.88	$3860.23	$3860.23

Year														
2008	1468.36	903.25	−38.49%	3.11%	$91.18	$72.03	15.00%	15.00%	$5.78	$522.55	$1824.54	$1918.30	$3860.23	$2440.84
2009	903.25	1115.10	23.45%	2.00%	$55.97	$44.22	15.00%	15.00%	$11.50	$1040.28	$1918.30	$2005.77	$2440.84	$3046.05
2010	1115.10	1257.64	12.78%	1.84%	$60.52	$47.81	15.00%	15.00%	$15.01	$1358.16	$2005.77	$2110.06	$3046.05	$3468.22
2011	1257.64	1257.60	0.00%	2.07%	$71.79	$56.71	15.00%	15.00%	$14.26	$1290.15	$2110.06	$2220.41	$3468.22	$3510.56
2012	1257.60	1426.19	13.41%	2.13%	$81.04	$64.02	15.00%	15.00%	$18.49	$1672.73	$2220.41	$2353.98	$3510.56	$4026.71
2013	1426.19	1848.36	29.60%	1.89%	$90.18	$45.63	23.80%	43.40%	$42.68	$2721.45	$2353.98	$2500.17	$4026.71	$5221.62
2014	1848.36	2058.90	11.39%	1.92%	$107.39	$54.34	23.80%	43.40%	$49.41	$3150.41	$2500.17	$2670.91	$5221.62	$5821.32
2015	2058.90	2043.94	−0.73%	2.11%	$122.27	$61.87	23.80%	43.40%	$46.31	$2952.71	$2670.91	$2841.87	$5821.32	$5794.58
2016	2043.94	2238.83	9.54%	2.01%	$123.41	$62.45	23.80%	43.40%	$52.23	$3329.96	$2841.87	$3027.35	$5794.58	$6357.31
2017	2238.83	2673.61	19.42%	1.87%	$133.31	$67.46	23.80%	43.40%	$68.01	$4336.32	$3027.35	$3255.02	$6357.31	$7591.35

Portfolio turnover

State tax	0%	10%	20%	30%	40%	50%	60%	70%	80%	90%	100%
0%	8.28%	7.40%	7.08%	6.87%	6.70%	6.53%	6.38%	6.21%	6.03%	5.86%	5.68%
1%	8.25%	7.33%	7.00%	6.78%	6.60%	6.43%	6.27%	6.09%	5.91%	5.73%	5.58%
2%	8.22%	7.26%	6.91%	6.69%	6.50%	6.33%	6.16%	5.97%	5.79%	5.60%	5.41%
3%	8.19%	7.19%	6.83%	6.60%	6.41%	6.22%	6.05%	5.86%	5.67%	5.47%	5.27%
4%	8.16%	7.12%	6.75%	6.51%	6.31%	6.12%	5.94%	5.74%	5.54%	5.34%	5.14%
5%	8.13%	7.05%	6.66%	6.41%	6.21%	6.01%	5.83%	5.62%	5.42%	5.21%	5.00%
6%	8.09%	6.98%	6.58%	6.32%	6.11%	5.91%	5.71%	5.51%	5.30%	5.08%	4.87%
7%	8.06%	6.91%	6.49%	6.23%	6.01%	5.80%	5.60%	5.39%	5.17%	4.95%	4.73%
8%	8.03%	6.83%	6.41%	6.14%	5.91%	5.70%	5.49%	5.27%	5.05%	4.83%	4.59%
9%	8.00%	6.76%	6.32%	6.04%	5.81%	5.59%	5.38%	5.16%	4.93%	4.69%	4.46%
10%	7.97%	6.69%	6.24%	5.95%	5.71%	5.49%	5.27%	5.04%	4.80%	4.56%	4.32%
11%	7.94%	6.61%	6.15%	5.86%	5.61%	5.38%	5.16%	4.92%	4.68%	4.43%	4.19%
12%	7.91%	6.54%	6.06%	5.76%	5.51%	5.28%	5.05%	4.81%	4.56%	4.30%	4.05%
13%	7.88%	6.47%	5.98%	5.67%	5.41%	5.17%	4.94%	4.69%	4.43%	4.17%	3.91%

5% turnover, 6% state + bracket, 0–13% state tax & 0–100% turnover

hypothetical model portfolio, an investor in the highest tax bracket who invested $100 on January 1, 1957. The stocks in the portfolio match the performance of the S&P 500 Index inclusive of dividends. The model portfolio's turnover rate is 5% for the base illustration. We also modeled for a 20% turnover rate, which we believe represents a "core" investment style for active managers. Note that the actual turnover rate of the S&P 500 is assumed to be 5% over the same period, and the turnover of the average actively managed mutual fund is assumed to be as high as 90%.

As we drilled down into more detail from the base model, we examined the variations in after-tax returns with turnover rates ranging from 0 to 100%. In each of the years, the portfolio paid taxes on dividends at the prevailing top tax rate, and all gains resulting from portfolio turnover were taxed at the prevailing long-term capital gains rates. The base model assumes a 6% state tax rate, but, as you will see, we also examined variations in state tax rates from 0 to 13%. As you will see, there is a remarkable variation in net returns earned on a portfolio owned by an investor domiciled in a no-tax state such as Florida and one living in a high-tax state such as California or New York.

The annualized, after-tax return for a high net worth investor who began investing in 1957 and who liquidated her portfolio on December 31, 2017, was 7.36%. To normalize for any long-term investment period since 1957, we analyzed each rolling 10- and 20-year period[3] and concluded that the average annualized return for a 10-year period was 7.40% and 7.97% for a 20-year period. The median returns for these two investment horizons are 6.77% and 7.65%, respectively.[4]

In the model, we simulated an actual portfolio with an initial $100 investment. The dividend yield during the first year was 1.75%. The S&P 500 dropped by 8.05% in 1957, and the annual dividend totaled $1.66, as a result of the declining value of the portfolio during the year. The tax on dividends in 1957 was 91% (the highest recorded taxation level), and we assumed a state tax of an additional 6%. After payment of federal and state taxes on dividends, the $1.66 was reduced to only $0.05. The portfolio turnover was assessed at a rate of 5%, which resulted in a capital gains tax loss carry-forward for the first year.

---

[3] Ten-year rolling returns studied 1957–1967, 1958–1968, and so on. Twenty-year rolling returns studied 1957–1977, 1958–1978, and so on.

[4] For rolling 10- and 20-year periods, we used the lower of "annual return" or "post liquidation."

Impact of State of Residence on After-Tax Returns

The investor or trust's state of residence has a notable effect on the long-term returns of equity portfolios because of variations in the rate of taxation on investment gains and dividends. In the above example, we modeled for a state income tax rate of 6% and concluded that the long-term compounded after-tax return of the equity portfolio was 7.36%. A portfolio that benefited from zero state tax in such states as Alaska, Florida, Nevada, South Dakota, Texas, Washington, or Wyoming would witness its annualized after-tax compounded return rise to 7.70%.

The zero-state-tax equity portfolio achieved an additional 34 basis points annualized return over the 6% state tax portfolio. Measured over many decades on a multimillion dollar portfolio, there is a significant capital accumulation advantage for the zero-state-tax portfolios.

As it happens, many portfolios of wealthy families are domiciled in high-income-tax states such as California with a 13.3% state tax, Vermont with an 8.95% state tax, Oregon with a 9.9% state tax, or the District of Columbia with an 8.95% tax. Investors living in New York City experience a combined city and state income tax rate of 12.7%. When we modeled the after-tax equity portfolio with a state tax rate of 13.3 (still using a turnover rate of 5%), the annualized return dropped to 6.92%. The difference between the zero-state-tax portfolios and the California portfolio was 78 basis points.

Impact of High Turnover Rates on Gross Returns

Portfolio turnover results in substantial costs to the investor. In building and studying the model, we observed portfolio turnover rates ranging from 0 to 100%. This allows those investors who prefer low-turnover equity portfolios to higher-turnover strategies to participate. Some investors opt for an equity mutual fund, and they will experience the fund's average turnover, which can be as high as 90%. In our view, the 20% turnover rate we used as the secondary benchmark in our model was appropriate based on observations of large capitalization "core" portfolios. Note, as you examine Table 11.1, how much variation exists in the after-tax returns of portfolios that had identical gross returns yet achieved markedly lower net results. Equally notable is the effect, positive and negative, that state taxes had on net returns under varying portfolio turnover rates:

- The most favorable return (8.28%) occurred in the portfolio with a 0% turnover rate domiciled in a 0% income tax state, and
- The least favorable return (3.91%) came from the portfolio with a 100% portfolio turnover rate (366-day holding period in order to qualify for long-term capital gains tax rates) domiciled in a 13% income tax state. This fact might give pause to even the most talented day traders.

The difference between these two portfolios is 4.37%, which, over several decades, would have significant accumulation implications on a multimillion dollar portfolio. In dollar terms, if the two portfolios were to begin with $100 million, the one with no state tax and no turnover costs would earn an additional $11.8 billion over the 61 years we studied.

The Role of Time Horizon as a Predictor of Investment Results

As we studied the model and adjusted for state income taxes and portfolio turnover rates, the more we felt compelled to study shorter time horizons to see if it was possible for us to spot patterns, trends, valuation ratios, and characteristics that would have been visible to an investor *before* deploying capital in a portfolio. As a result of this analysis, we found convincing evidence that the most reliable time horizon for equity portfolios is 20 years because of the high correlation rate between earnings yield and rolling 20-year compounded performance. We also believe that 20-year observation periods give the investor a basis for comparing equities to the Bond Buyer 20 General Obligation Bond Index (which has an average maturity of 20 years). We discussed in detail in Chap. 7 the utility of using earnings yield in assessing the long-term return of equities. In observing the earnings yield of the portfolio in each year and the corresponding annualized returns the portfolio would achieve for each rolling 20-year period, we found a 0.79 correlation with the after-tax return the portfolio ultimately would achieve at the end of that same period.

The 10-year returns were more volatile than the 20-year periods, with a correlation rate of 0.61 between the earnings yield at the beginning of each 10-year rolling period and the after-tax return the portfolio would ultimately achieve at the end of that same period.

These data points prove that the effect of P/E ratio expansion and contraction has such a strong impact on actual returns over short time periods (such as 10 years) that simple valuation observations become less reliable predictive tools. As a result, it became clear that the earnings yield, with a few exceptions, was one of the best predictors of future returns on an after-tax basis (see Table 11.2).

Table 11.2 Twenty-year equity rolling returns (1957–2017)

Time period	2-year. annualized return	Beginning of period (Jan 1)	
Beginning (Jan)–End (Dec)	After tax, 5% turnover	P/E	Earnings yield
1957–1976	4.45%	13.3×	7.52%
1958–1977	4.23%	11.9×	8.40%
1959–1978	2.97%	19.1×	5.24%
1960–1979	3.41%	17.7×	5.65%
1961–1980	4.61%	18.7×	5.35%
1962–1981	3.20%	21.2×	4.72%
1963–1982	4.50%	17.2×	5.81%
1964–1983	4.63%	18.2×	5.49%
1965–1984	4.24%	17.8×	5.62%
1966–1985	5.13%	17.4×	5.75%
1967–1986	6.47%	14.9×	6.71%
1968–1987	5.77%	17.7×	5.65%
1969–1988	6.06%	18.2×	5.49%
1970–1989	7.94%	15.1×	6.62%
1971–1990	7.62%	16.7×	5.99%
1972–1991	8.40%	18.3×	5.46%
1973–1992	7.94%	19.1×	5.24%
1974–1993	9.25%	12.3×	8.13%
1975–1994	10.83%	7.3×	13.70%
1976–1995	11.08%	11.7×	8.55%
1977–1996	11.18%	11.0×	9.09%
1978–1997	13.22%	8.8×	11.36%
1979–1998	14.42%	8.3×	12.05%
1980–1999	14.75%	7.4×	13.51%
1981–2000	12.88%	9.1×	10.99%
1982–2001	12.55%	8.1×	12.35%
1983–2002	10.33%	10.2×	9.80%
1984–2003	10.72%	12.4×	8.06%
1985–2004	11.05%	9.9×	10.10%
1986–2005	9.99%	13.5×	7.41%
1987–2006	9.98%	16.8×	5.95%
1988–2007	10.03%	15.4×	6.49%
1989–2008	6.87%	11.5×	8.70%
1990–2009	6.79%	14.5×	6.90%
1991–2010	7.68%	14.6×	6.85%
1992–2011	6.52%	21.6×	4.63%
1993–2012	6.95%	20.9×	4.78%
1994–2013	7.93%	17.3×	5.78%
1995–2014	8.51%	14.5×	6.91%
1996–2015	7.00%	16.3×	6.12%
1997–2016	6.54%	18.2×	5.49%
1998–2017	6.14%	22.0×	4.54%

Correlation 0.79

In examining 20-year periods we found:

- The lowest after-tax return for equities of any 20-year period began on January 1, 1959, and ended on December 31, 1978. The annualized return for this period was 2.97%.
- The highest after-tax return of any 20-year period began on January 1, 1980, and ended on December 31, 1999. The annualized return for this period was 14.75%.
- The average after-tax return for all 20-year rolling periods was 7.97; the median was 7.65%.

We thought the period from 1989 to 2008 was particularly interesting. Despite the fact that there were three recessions (1991, 2000, and 2008) and two bear markets each representing a nearly 50% loss (2000 to 2002 and 2008 to 2009), the annualized return for a portfolio that began on January 1, 1989, and was liquidated on December 31, 2008, was 6.87%. When reviewing the 20-year returns, the bull market that ended around 2000 stands out because the after-tax returns for periods beginning between 1978 and 1982 all exceeded 12.00%.

Upon inspection of the wide variations in the results of various vintages, we asked ourselves, what statistics were available to investors at the beginning of these periods that would have given clues to the ultimate return that would be earned over the 20-year periods? Our objective in studying this history was to extract statistics that would have been available to investors that would have enabled them to make informed decisions about the future returns of their portfolios and whether stocks or bonds would outperform the other over various periods (we will discuss this question in detail later in the chapter). Future rates of inflation, GDP growth, earnings growth, and multiple expansions/contractions are not easily predicted by an investor beginning a 20-year investment portfolio. Another unknown is the ultimate tax rate that will be in effect for the next 20 years, so the investor must choose between modeling the current tax rate or an estimated tax rate. Investors in 2001 might rightfully have estimated that portfolio taxation rates would be lower in the future given the Bush administration's emphasis on removing or reducing the double taxation of dividends. Similarly, an investor in the early 1960s would have been justified in modeling a lower forward-looking tax rate, given President Kennedy's insistence that the 91% top rate of taxation was a drag on the economy and, as he neared the end of his first term, acceptance of the idea was gaining momentum. The earnings yield (trailing 12-month earnings/price) is the one statistic that might have given investors a clue as to the actual after-tax return of their portfolios at the time of investment.

The Role of Time Horizon on Decision to Liquidate a Portfolio

As important as the year in which investors begin investing in equities is the year in which they liquidate their investments. Using ten-year investment periods as an example, an investor who started on January 1, 1991, and liquidated on December 31, 2000, achieved a 13.55% return, whereas an investor who began on January 1, 1993, and liquidated on December 31, 2002, achieved a 6.99% return (nearly 50% lower). The two investors shared eight years in which they received the same returns, but during the two years they did not, 2001 and 2002, the S&P declined by 13.04% and 23.37%, respectively.

The temptation to liquidate a portfolio after sub-par returns can eliminate a large portion of the gains experienced in the previous years. For example, if the investor who began in 1993 had waited another two years, his annualized return after taxes would have increased to 8.55%. It must be noted that ordinary income taxes and capital gains taxes were reduced during year 12, which, of course, affected the final liquidation return; however, even without the tax change he still would have gained. I use this example to illustrate the fact that bear markets and recessions can inflict a bigger hit on 10-year than on 20-year holding periods. The 1983–2002 vintage portfolio managed to produce an after-tax return of 10.33% despite the fact that the last year of the portfolio witnessed the trough of a 50% bear market.

After-Tax Impact on the Decision to Invest in Bonds versus Equities

The after-tax equity risk premium over municipal bonds from 1957 to 2017 was 1.83%. Comparing the 20-year return data with the *Bond Buyer Index* (also known as the *Bond Buyer Index of 20 Year General Obligation Bonds*) yield over a similar time period, we found the average equity premium was 2.01% with a median of 1.38%. Of the 42 rolling 20-year periods we studied, there were seven in which bonds outperformed equities. The first occurred during the 20-year period beginning in 1959 and ending in 1978. The bond portfolio would have returned 3.40%, while the equity portfolio returned 2.97%. The largest period of bond outperformance was 1982 to 2001. During this period, the bond portfolio returned 13.36%, and the equity portfolio returned 12.55% for a total outperformance of 81 basis points.

The largest period of equity outperformance was 1979 to 1998. In that period the bond portfolio returned 6.58%, and the equity portfolio returned 14.42% for a total equity outperformance of 7.84%. Another interesting observation giving further evidence of the link between earnings yield and future returns, the earnings yield of the equity portfolio in 1979 was 12.05%. That earnings yield was a predictor of the 20-year after-tax performance that followed resulting in a difference of 240 basis points 12.05% earnings yield versus 14.45% actual performance.

In order to compare the annualized compounded after-tax returns of the equity portfolio, we decided to illustrate a best- and worst-case municipal bond portfolio. While the straight-line average of the *Bond Buyer Index* from 1957 to 2017 was 5.52% (straight-line average of bond buyer yields Table 11.3), we wanted to illustrate the effect that the timing of bond purchases would have had on a real-life portfolio. Therefore, we created 20 different municipal bond portfolios, each with different starting years to minimize the impact of the yields at the time a new bond was purchased. The best-case portfolio had a compounded after-tax return of 7.6% (meaning that the bonds outperformed equities by 1.36%) and the worst-case portfolio had a 4.5% compounded return (meaning that equities outperformed bonds by 1.74%).

We requested input on our study from the investor and investment management communities, and many suggested that we examine an actively managed municipal bond portfolio or mutual fund that could be compared to the simulated portfolios of rolling 20-year *Bond Buyer 20 Index* returns. This was a good suggestion, and we decided to analyze hypothetical returns from the T Rowe Price Tax Exempt Municipal Bond Fund (an open-ended mutual fund containing a portfolio of municipal bonds that began on October 26, 1976).

Using the Morningstar Advisor Workstation, we modeled a hypothetical investment in the fund, (ticker PRTAX) with no sales load and re-investment of all dividend and capital gains distributions. From the initial investment at the inception of the fund on October 26, 1976, through year end December 31, 2017, the annualized return was 6%. Note that although the T Rowe fund does not does not go back as far as 1957 (the inception date of the S&P 500 Index), the returns of this portfolio even inclusive of fees tend to rhyme with our observation of the average yield of the *Bond Buyer Index*, which was 6.05%. Thus, an actively managed strategy investing in municipal bonds managed to achieve the average yields of the index over the same period. We felt it was necessary to address this point as early critics of our paper felt that observing the average yield of the index did not

Table 11.3 Bond buyer versus 20-year equity rolling returns

Time period	20-year bond buyer yield from Jan 1 beginning of year	20-year annualized return after tax	Outperformance	Equity premium	Missed prediction	Beginning-of-year earnings yield
1958–1977	2.97%	4.23%	Equities	1.26%		8.40%
1959–1978	3.40%	2.97%	**Bonds**	−0.43%	x	5.24%
1960–1979	3.78%	3.41%	**Bonds**	−0.37%	x	5.65%
1961–1980	3.39%	4.61%	Equities	1.22%		5.35%
1962–1981	3.37%	3.20%	**Bonds**	−0.17%	x	4.72%
1963–1982	3.05%	4.50%	Equities	1.45%		5.81%
1964–1983	3.26%	4.63%	Equities	1.37%		5.49%
1965–1984	3.07%	4.24%	Equities	1.17%		5.62%
1966–1985	3.53%	5.13%	Equities	1.60%		5.75%
1967–1986	3.76%	6.47%	Equities	2.71%		6.71%
1968–1987	4.38%	5.77%	Equities	1.39%		5.65%
1969–1988	4.85%	6.06%	Equities	1.21%		5.49%
1970–1989	6.61%	7.94%	Equities	1.33%		6.62%
1971–1990	5.74%	7.62%	Equities	1.88%		5.99%
1972–1991	5.03%	8.40%	Equities	3.37%		5.46%
1973–1992	5.08%	7.94%	Equities	2.86%		5.24%
1974–1993	5.18%	9.25%	Equities	4.07%		8.13%
1975–1994	7.08%	10.83%	Equities	3.75%		13.70%
1976–1995	7.13%	11.08%	Equities	3.95%		8.55%
1977–1996	5.78%	11.18%	Equities	5.40%		9.09%
1978–1997	5.64%	13.22%	Equities	7.58%		11.36%
1979–1998	6.58%	14.42%	Equities	7.84%		12.05%
1980–1999	7.32%	14.75%	Equities	7.43%		13.51%
1981–2000	9.49%	12.88%	Equities	3.39%		10.99%
1982–2001	13.36%	12.55%	**Bonds**	−0.81%		12.35%
1983–2002	9.48%	10.33%	Equities	0.85%		9.80%
1984–2003	9.66%	10.72%	Equities	1.06%	x	8.06%
1985–2004	9.87%	11.05%	Equities	1.18%		10.10%
1986–2005	8.33%	9.99%	Equities	1.66%	x	7.41%
1987–2006	6.70%	9.98%	Equities	3.28%	x	5.95%
1988–2007	7.83%	10.03%	Equities	2.20%	x	6.49%
1989–2008	7.44%	6.87%	**Bonds**	−0.57%	x	8.70%
1990–2009	7.03%	6.79%	**Bonds**	−0.24%		6.90%
1991–2010	7.09%	7.68%	Equities	0.59%	x	6.85%
1992–2011	6.52%	6.52%	**Bonds**	0.00%		4.63%
1993–2012	6.17%	6.95%	Equities	0.78%	x	4.78%
1994–2013	5.34%	7.93%	Equities	2.59%		5.78%
1995–2014	6.66%	8.51%	Equities	1.85%		6.91%
1996–2015	5.37%	7.00%	Equities	1.63%		6.12%
1997–2016	5.70%	6.54%	Equities	0.84%	x	5.49%
1998–2017	5.07%	6.14%	Equities	1.07%	x	4.54%

account for the impact of bonds called prior to maturity or lengthening or shortening of maturities over time.

It should be noted that the starting yield to maturity of a 20-year bond can be achieved only if the bond is non-callable (therefore capable of experiencing 20 years of coupon income), if the re-invested coupon income achieves an identical yield as the starting yield, and if the bond experiences no default in terms of missed coupon payments or principal returned to the investor at maturity.

We found that while yield to maturity is one of the most important variables considered by investors considering purchase, it is rarely achieved in reality. Bond investors would find it impossible to achieve the exact same re-investment yield in each year of a 20-year bond due to the natural fluctuation of interest rates. In addition, most general obligation coupon bonds have some degree of callability. Thus, the only real-life way to achieve a known long-term compounding rate is to purchase a non-callable home state zero coupon bond. Zero coupon bonds are priced at a discount to maturity value and, when purchased and redeemed at par, will experience the exact annualized compounded yield to maturity that appears on the purchase confirmation. Figure 11.1 shows the dollar compounding of an equity portfolio matching the performance of the S&P 500 Index (pre-tax), an equity portfolio matching the S&P 500 Index (after subtracting prevailing dividend and capital gains taxes), and a tax-free municipal bond portfolio matching the yield of the Bond Buyer 20 General Obligation Index.

The 1957–2017 study produced many interesting results:

- Twenty-year rolling returns are the most reliable measurement period for both stock and bond portfolios.
- The average equity premium (on a 5% turnover portfolio) over tax-exempt municipal bonds was 2.01%.

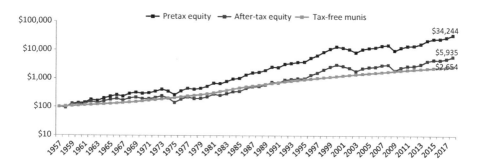

Fig. 11.1 Growth of $100 (1957–2017)

- Earnings yield provided a 0.79 correlation to the actual after-tax return earned by investors over 20-year periods.
- Tax-exempt bond portfolios outperformed equity portfolios in 17% of the rolling 20-year periods (7 out of 42).
- A general correlation was observed between tax-exempt bond yields and the after-tax returns of equity portfolios over 20-year rolling periods.
- High-turnover portfolios matching the performance of the S&P 500 Index and domiciled in high-income-tax states have under-performed municipal bonds after taxes and fees.

As you can see from all this data, for the high net worth investor there is a massive disparity between pre-tax and after-tax returns, which has a cumulative impact on the dollar compounding of a portfolio over time. As an individual investor, it is important that you grasp the idea that for taxable investors the spread between equity and fixed income returns is narrower than the spread for non-taxable portfolios. Thus, you must (from the inception of your portfolio) measure the potential outperformance of a stock portfolio, estimate the loss of return as a result of taxes, and make a reasonable comparison between the forward-looking returns of various asset classes.

12

Building Your Investment Team

A wealth management team should begin with your CIO or wealth advisor. Once you have appointed this person, you should round out the team with a trusted estate planning attorney, a certified public accountant (CPA) or a tax professional, a successor trustee, along with various "as needed" vendors and professionals hired for specific short-term tasks along the way.

Deciding How to Invest: Do-It-Yourself versus Fund Manager versus Financial Advisor

Before embarking on the task of hiring an advisor, some introspection is required to determine whether you desire or need one in the first place.

Do-It-Yourself Investor

Do-it-yourself (or self-directed) investors must immerse themselves in the finer points of investing, which include:

- Evaluating the relative worth of the equity and bond markets. They will need that for the first asset allocation decision.
- Knowing how to look for periods when the equity risk premium goes negative, prompting the decision to overweight bonds, and then, when conditions warrant, deciding to reverse this stance.

© The Author(s) 2019
N. J. Gannon, *Tailored Wealth Management*,
https://doi.org/10.1007/978-3-319-99780-3_12

- Ascertaining the relative valuation of the major world economies and their stock markets and currency.
- Understanding the various methodologies for calculating qualitative metrics such as P/E ratios or book value that are used by different index sponsors such as Standard & Poor's, Russell, and others.
- Determining whether their chosen index fund strategy will be market capitalization weighted or equal weighted. The market capitalization weighted index weights the companies in the index by their size. In this scenario, the dollars allocated to Google dwarf those allocated to a company like Big Lots. In an equal weighted fund each of the companies in the index receives the same amount of investment dollars.

Do-it-yourself investors will need to get their decisions right on these inflection points, and should take their time and study these important topics before putting a single dollar at risk. This may seem like a lot for the individual investor to shoulder, but some have the temperament and knowledge to succeed doing it this way. To quote the iconic Canadian rock band Rush, "If you choose not to decide you still have made a choice."

A major drawback of the self-directed model is that the surviving spouse will have to start at square one if the self-directing spouse is the pre-decedent. There is a price to pay for continuity and those who choose to self-direct must have a contingency plan in place that involves the input of the spouse or family so that when they are called upon to take over these functions, they will have a plan to do so.

Fund Manager

For investors choosing to outsource the task of asset allocation and security selection to a professional fund manager, I strongly suggest that they select a balanced global strategy where the manager has the discretion to own equities and fixed income in the same portfolio. There are a handful of these organizations that have 40+-year track records that you can study and evaluate. At least two such funds began before the stock market crash of 1929, so they are fine examples of track records over the long haul. If you find a fund where there is a repeatable process or ethos that governs the portfolio, you won't worry when one member of the investment team retires or leaves the firm.

Financial Advisor

For investors choosing to go with a financial advisor, there are two things that are critical to your success: (1) finding an advisor with whom you have a genuine chemistry, one with whom you feel you will be able to build a relationship; and (2) choosing an advisor who is able to explain in language that YOU understand how they intend to protect and build your capital. Early in the process, it is very easy to meet someone and immediately trust them. Resist the temptation. Do your due diligence. TAKE YOUR TIME in formulating your plan. This is especially important for those of you who are recently divorced or have lost the spouse who made all the financial decisions.

Make sure to ask the advisor about their mother's portfolio—what it is invested in, whether she has a mortgage or not. A very easy question to ask the advisor is, "At what interest rate would you advise me to put my entire portfolio into treasury bonds or FDIC insured CDs?" There must be a number where every investor or advisor says to themselves, "If I could earn ____ in low risk, long-term bonds I would do it." You'll get interesting answers to this question when interviewing potential candidates.

A financial advisor may be the family's highest-paid vendor. It is essential that you understand whether the fees you are charged add value. It is also important for you to be able to differentiate the fees that go toward straight money management and those that compensate your advisor for her time in performing non-financial holistic tasks. Too often, the advisor hides behind low-fee index funds or ETFs and marries the strategy with an expensive financial planning fee. It is perfectly reasonable for you to compensate your advisor, just don't over-pay and certainly don't over-pay to the point where they challenge your net portfolio returns. The advisors who made billions in fees while the pension fund shortfall ballooned to $4 trillion certainly did not give their clients their money's worth.

How to Select a Financial Advisor

The question "how to select a financial advisor?" elicited "about 3,610,000 results (0.77 seconds)" on Google. Before we get into details of what you should be looking for, I must emphatically say that you will need to engage both sides of your brain to settle on an outcome that you can live with for decades. You may determine that the right person must be someone who gives you a gut feeling about their appropriateness, someone with whom you may feel a personal chemistry. That's fine as long as you do not breach your duty to assiduously scour the numbers necessary to make the right decision.

Striking the right balance may be difficult, but stay on task! There is no rush to make a decision until you are comfortable. If an advisor signals that there is an opportunity you might miss out on by delaying, strike that candidate from your list.

I have mentioned Charlotte Beyer, founder of the IPI, several times. Charlotte authored *Wealth Management Unwrapped* (2017, Wiley) in which she addresses the financial advisor question in plain English in an easily consumable format. I'll add my voice to the reviews applauding this easy read, which, I believe, should be assigned to all wealth creators looking for an advisor.

Types of Financial Advisors

There are several categories into which financial advisors fall. We shall address the pros and cons of each:

The In-Sourced or Outsourced CIO Model: An in-sourced CIO is one that you hire who has full discretion to make financial decisions on your behalf. The professional might be a family office executive to whom you pay a salary (in-sourced) OR she might be the managing director of a boutique money management firm (outsourced) that caters to a handful of families like yours. A family office executive might be a seasoned investment professional in whom you have a high level of trust and confidence to make portfolio and asset allocation decisions on your behalf. If you look at some of the successful college endowment portfolios, you will see that they employ the in-sourced CIO model where a seasoned professional oversees a team of strategists and portfolio managers to implement their mandate to beat or achieve the organization's investment goals.

As a wealthy family, you may hire a boutique investment firm that operates not as an investment consultant, but one who is given discretion to make direct investment decisions on your behalf. I would like to see more firms adopt this model, as I believe that when operated effectively they can control fees, provide an understanding of the assets owned by the family, offer a sharp focus and concentration, and won't fall victim to over-diversification or mediocrity. If you are wondering whether an advisor might be considered for the position of outsourced CIO, ask this handful of questions at the inception of the relationship:

- What percentage of your firm's assets will my family represent?
- How many families does your firm represent and is there a limit to how many you will represent before closing to new relationships?
- Does your firm claim compliance with the Global Investment Performance Standards, and is there an outside audit that verifies your performance record?
- Does your fee schedule change from client to client or do you offer your most competitive fee arrangement to all relationships?
- Will my investment decisions be outsourced to other firms, ETFs, mutual funds, or are all investment decisions implemented internally?
- Are your investment results reported gross or net of taxes?
- To continue my due diligence, may I have several references from people who are in similar financial situations to mine (people whose contact information the advisor is willing to share)?

The Private Wealth Advisor: A second model of private wealth advisor is the investment consultant. This model mirrors (in many ways) the institutional model of endowments and private foundations. An investment consultant, unlike the outsourced CIO, will act as a quarterback. You will pay a fee to the consultant based upon assets under management for asset allocation advice, manager selection, and portfolio monitoring. With an investment consultant model, money management decisions are delegated to other money managers, ETFs, mutual funds, and private investments. The consultant can be found in large private wealth trust companies, the major Wall Street Private Wealth Management firms, and some consulting firms that serve both private investors and institutional clients.

For families with over $100 million under management, the fee paid to the investment consultant will likely be smaller than the cumulative fees of the outsourced money managers. Those who favor this model like the fact that the investment consultant can recommend that you deploy capital virtually anywhere. Their job is to search for funds and investment managers who fit the required asset allocation sleeve, monitor their progress, and make recommendations going forward.

Some investors find that a consultant-advised portfolio is so broadly diversified by asset class, manager, and securities that it becomes difficult to decipher that which will ultimately build or destroy capital in the portfolio. That is, if the performance of a portfolio is a function of the success of the individual investments it contains, an investor or their consultant might not be able to address questions about individual securities or the risks they contain. When the sun is shining on a bull market, questions about the thickness of the castle walls in a portfolio are less common than when markets are succumbing to major corrections or crashes.

It is difficult for a consultant to offer a prospective new client a comprehensive audited performance track record. In their defense, institutional and private wealth clients may have very different asset allocations and a widely varied team of outside money managers. However, consultants will often provide prospective clients with a "representative list" of clients that might offer insight into their particular asset allocations and performance data. These performance numbers may not be indicative of what the new client portfolio will look like, but it can provide the basis for an intelligent discussion about changes and inflection points over the history of the account. It is also common for the representative client list to include references the prospective client may contact.

Additional Skills to Look for in a Financial Advisor

An effective financial advisor must display skills and experience that go beyond investing and monitoring the family's financial capital. He or she must understand the nuances of the family's estate plan. It is also critical for them to understand the philanthropic intent and social capital of the family. In short, the family should be certain that when the death of the wealth creator occurs, the beneficiaries will feel confident that their advisor will take a holistic and comprehensive view of the task ahead. Ideally, the advisor will benefit from the cumulative experience gained by having worked with the family for decades.

How to Select the Other Teammates

We have discussed the components of the in-sourced and outsourced CIO, the investment consultant, the fund manager, and the self-directed investor. Now let's talk about the other players that form a comprehensive wealth management team:

- Trusted family attorney
- Family office executive: Do you need one or not?
- CPA or tax attorney
- Executive director of your family foundation or donor-advised fund
- Insurance professional

- Philanthropy manager, educational peer group, and other à la carte professionals

Note: Referrals from friends and business associates you admire are often the best source for finding these professionals.

Family Attorney

Every family should have a trusted legal advisor for those items that require planning (such as estate planning and gifting) as well as those that cannot be anticipated (such as litigation defense or plaintiff work, the sudden death of a family member), real estate contracts, and other items whose magnitude warrants a trained legal eye.

The topic on which you'll likely spend most of your time with your legal advisor is estate planning. For most couples the first trip to the attorney is to establish their wills, and, as a rule, the item of highest importance is the selection of a guardian for minor children. We cover the nuances of estate planning in Chap. 16. Very often, the couple continues to patronize the same attorney for subsequent matters such as durable powers of attorney and healthcare directives (often referred to as "living wills").

It is wonderful when a family finds the right person—someone with whom they can travel throughout the journey—for the very first task, establishing the first estate plan and the subsequent documents that arise in families with complex issues. As the family matures, the trusted attorney knows all of the nuances of the documents that are in place and the decisions that were made to get to that place. An experienced attorney will have had myriad experiences with his or her clients ranging from those who strive for complexity to those who care very little about the process of estate and estate tax planning.

In choosing your attorney, it is important to remember you aren't just paying for the time and advice they deliver to produce your documents, but for the cumulative experience they have had with other clients. Estate planning attorneys often are the first to hear of tectonic shifts that may take place in a wealthy family. For example, they may hear statements like these:

- "I've decided to take the giving pledge and give 50% of my wealth to charity during my lifetime and when I die. Once I do, this will be a part of the public record."

- "My husband and I have decided to take our $11 million estate tax exemption and gift $1 million each to each of our siblings and their spouses, and set up 529 plans for all of the nieces and nephews."
- "I am donating my body to medical research after my death."
- "Carol and I have decided to get a divorce."
- "My daughter hasn't picked up the phone to call me in five years. I'm writing her out of my estate."
- "I have decided that any beneficiary of a trust in which I am the grantor must have a prenuptial agreement in place before a wedding."
- "I have decided to divest myself of our diversified portfolio and build another company."
- "I have decided to sell the family business."
- "I would like to establish a family partnership in order to pass assets on to my heirs with a minimal loss of capital to estate taxes."

These are just a handful of examples of discussions you may first have with your trusted attorney. He or she may not personally be an expert in the subcategory of law that addresses the individual issue, but will be the quarterback who ensures that the right person is put in place. I strongly advise that you take your time until you find a person with whom you have personal chemistry. Recently, I have seen a designated legal representative granted the authority (within a trust document) to appoint his or her successor.

What to Look for in a Family Office Executive

Before you look, first ask yourself, "Do I need one?"

"Family office" has become a buzzword in the wealth management business. Most firms who use the term are hoping that you decide NOT to open a family office and instead hire them with their suite of "family office type" products and services. A family office certainly can make sense when the assets of the family exceed $500 million and coordination and documentation can be not only cost justified, but also necessary for the execution and continuity of estate and gifting plans.

The individuals you consider should be highly credentialed, experienced, and capable of managing a growing team of professionals. It is beneficial, but not necessary, for the executive to have a personal history with the family's operating business.

What to Look for in a CPA

The family CPA is more important to the family than the routine fling with the IRS form 1040. The CPA will likely be included in the circle of trusted advisors called upon to perform in a "board of directors" capacity for major inflection points in the management of the family's estate and properties. These days, it is common for CPAs to be copied as interested parties on brokerage, custodian statements in addition to 1099s and K-1s needed for annual tax filings. If your wealth advisor and CPA work together collaboratively, they will have conversations or communication throughout the year that will inform each of them about such items as tax losses carry forward, realized gains for the year, the presence of charitable gifts carry forward, payment schedules for estimated taxes, and the acquisition of tax credits (in states where this is practiced).

While the year end 2017 tax reform eliminated items such as miscellaneous tax deductions and unreimbursed employee business expenses, your CPA should be skilled in communicating the habits and the decisions made in the preparation of tax documents as well as any advice he or she provides. There seems to be a polarized view about the nature of the advice—usually about how aggressive to be in taking tax deductions—that a CPA must give his client. I understand why someone would want an aggressive CPA. Indeed, clients seem to favor accountants who strive to ensure that every item that could qualify as a deduction is deducted. But it seems to me that regardless of whether or not one chooses to pursue politics later in life, an embarrassment resulting from aggressive or even fraudulent tax filings falls under the category: just not worth it.

So, instead of looking for an aggressive CPA, I recommend seeking someone who is well informed, someone in whom you can have confidence, someone who will communicate messages such as these:

- "I see that you have been writing larger and more frequent checks for charitable causes. It may be time to discuss the donation of appreciated securities that could allow your charities to get a bigger bang for the buck."
- "It may now be the time for you to take the loss on that business you invested in that failed a few years ago. In that way, it can offset future capital gains."
- "Our state offers taxpayers the opportunity to fund their state tax liability at 91–94 cents on the dollar using state tax credits. While there are some

limited risks that you should consider, is this something you would like me to research for you?"

- "I received notice from the IRS that you are being audited for tax year 2016. Do not worry. I have the documentation necessary to represent you in this matter. I will keep you informed."

A final word of advice about selecting your CPA. Don't be a cheapskate. The fees for preparing tax documents are minimal in comparison to the tax liability they will verify. You should encourage your CPA to collaborate with your attorney and financial advisor when appropriate even though you will incur additional fees. Last, don't cut your CPA out of the loop when making far-reaching planning decisions.

What to Look for in an Executive Director of a Family Foundation or Donor-Advised Fund

If your family has put a significant focus on philanthropy, your family foundation will drive this process. Large foundations (those that exceed $100 million in assets) may employ an executive director to oversee asset management, grant applications, payment of awards, publicity surrounding foundation specific projects, and the annual IRS 990 filing that will ultimately be available to the public.

A 2014 article in the *Chronicle of Philanthropy* reported that the median salary for a full-time position at a grant-making organization was $74,061. The median salary for chief executive officers of foundations was reported to be $156,733. The high range for CEOs was $600,000 for foundations with $2 billion or more in assets to a low range of $90,000 for organizations with $10 million or less. Families should be careful if they choose to hire a family member to take a paid role on the family foundation's staff; that number will be made public and may be scrutinized if it is excessive.

Some family foundations, in my opinion, have become less effective as years pass after the death of the founder. I have seen family foundations that have 50 pages of grants of $1000 to $5000 per grantee that seem to have no specific focus or guiding principle. Successful foundations that operate under the management of an effective executive director enjoy the advocacy of someone who is committed to the founder's original intent, is excited about engaging younger members of the family through participation in the grant-making process, and understands the embarrassment that can result when the foundation fails in a public way.

After the death of the wealth creator or founder, many families feel that they would benefit from the guidance of an executive director whose efforts will maximize positive outcomes. In addition to the obvious experience you would want to see on the résumé of a candidate, a personal history with the wealth creator would be a significant plus. Of course, your family foundation's executive director and its trustees will be bound by the bylaws under which it operates, but one of the most important ethical considerations steering decisions and inflection points should be founder's intent. It is essential, therefore, to find people committed to, where possible, discerning the founder's wishes when it comes to major points of policy that will affect the foundation's giving or its long-term impact.

What to Look for in an Insurance Broker and Agent

The complexities of insuring all of a wealthy family's risks makes finding a one-stop insurance advisor next to impossible. Wealthy families will carry homeowners insurance on their home(s) and automobiles. Coastal properties might have separate wind and flood coverage. They are likely to have an excess liability or umbrella insurance policy that covers financial losses that are exceeded by their home and auto lines. They will carry disability insurance if they are still engaged in an operating business. Families that own private aircraft will have separate coverage for that asset while those that own a yacht will have yet another policy that covers the vessel, crew, and passengers.

They may have a life insurance agent who coordinates complex insurance trusts that exist for the benefit of yet unborn members of the family. When they are young and middle-aged, they will need health insurance for themselves and their families, often covered by their companies or their employer's company. While Cadillac healthcare policies exist for those who wish to pay for them, for those who are older, there is Medicare, and I can say that I have been positively surprised at the satisfaction of elderly families who use it. So far, no complaints have risen to the level where they warrant inclusion here.

In observing of wealthy families, I have found that, because of its complexity, insurance is more likely to be negatively affected through oversight than many other things they have to consider. The simplest method to self-organize is with an Excel spreadsheet showing every property, carrier, annual premium, policy number and anniversary date, amount of deductible, and agents' contact information, among others. Families with multiple residences, aircraft, real estate, and yachts would do well to delegate this task to the family office executive.

What to Look for in a Philanthropy Manager and Other À la Carte Professionals

I address methods of structuring a family's philanthropic plan in Chap. 15; for now, it is important to know whether the management of the family foundation is going to be handled by your team of wealth advisors, self-managed by members of the family, or outsourced to a paid executive director (which might be considered for foundations exceeding $50 million in assets).

Other professionals that a family might choose to have on retainer include a private security firm that oversees the physical security and monitoring of the family residences, yachts, and aircraft. While this may sound overly cautious, I have met families who have placed professional security firms on retainer whose charge goes as far as orchestrating hostage extraction operations around the world, especially if the family travels to regions of the world where local law enforcement might not be trustworthy. Having a large amount of personal wealth carries new types of risks that should at least be reviewed as often as the family estate plan (usually every three to five years).

Families with an extensive art or musical instrument, antiquities, or wine collection may want to consider hiring a professional on retainer for annual reviews, insurance updates, to ensure the physical protection of the assets. For their fine arts, instruments, and antiques they might seek the services of a museum or experienced curator. If you own complex and valuable physical assets, they should be treated and thought of with the same risk management mentality that you would your financial investment portfolio and other valuable possessions.

The Last Step in the Selection Process

Your wealth management team should be comprehensive enough to meet your family's needs. Ask yourself and your most trusted and respected inner circle a series of "what if" questions and see if your plan addresses the things that are important to you. Remember also, the team you build to help you manage wealth should reduce, not add, the stress in your life.

13

Educational Resources for Investors

Critical thinking, curiosity, and a healthy dose of skepticism are necessary traits of a successful long-term investor. While gut feeling when making decisions is significant and good judgment about the trustworthiness of an advisor is also important, I must stress that an educated, broad perspective on wealth and its meaning *cannot* and *should not* be outsourced to an advisor. For those inclined to read, as you are now, there are a handful of classics that you should not neglect because that will lay the groundwork for this book and any new title to hit the shelves.

The Value of a Great Book

Two books were of monumental importance to me as an investor. In mid-1998, I attended an investment lecture in which the presenter mentioned John Kenneth Galbraith's *A Short History of Financial Euphoria*. In 1998, the US stock market was in the third year of an incredible bull market. Investors had shrugged off Federal Reserve Board Chairman Alan Greenspan's "Irrational Exuberance" speech of December 1996 and, at the time of this lecture, it seemed as if nothing would stop the bull in its tracks. Galbraith's illuminating book through stories, in very conversational prose, summarized and explained the causes of the events that led to the 1987 stock market crash, the seventeenth-century tulip bubble and collapse, the twentieth-century scheme of Charles Ponzi, among many others. This very easy read weaved a similar theme around financial collapses throughout the centuries. For example,

© The Author(s) 2019
N. J. Gannon, *Tailored Wealth Management*,
https://doi.org/10.1007/978-3-319-99780-3_13

investors didn't fully understand what they owned—neither stocks nor commodities. All they knew was that the price kept going up and so they were impelled to participate.

My own concern about equity valuations intensified in the summer of 1999 when the US tech bubble was inflating rapidly, taking with it the valuations of non-tech companies like Coca-Cola and General Electric. P/E ratios sported levels that had never before been seen, even surpassing the levels of September 1929. The financial media paraded bullish Wall Street strategists to their sets as quickly as they could unload the limos outside of their studios. Harry Dent's book *The Great Boom Ahead* flew off the shelves.

I was fortunate to work across the street from a now-shuttered bookstore called The Library Limited. One afternoon in June 1999, I was compelled to purchase a copy of Benjamin Graham and David Dodd's investment classic, *Security Analysis* (1934 edition). The book is very technical, but a look at the chart in the Introduction of the Dow Jones Industrial Average from 1906 to 1934 was sobering. The authors explained that stock prices, P/E ratios, and interest rates were important variables that would allow the investor to properly weight assets in a portfolio. I don't know what stroke of luck caused me to buy that book; I do know that it gave me actionable ideas, which, at that time, were to increase fixed income and decrease equity weightings in portfolios. The book, now in its sixth edition, had been on the shelves of libraries for 65 years by the time I purchased it, and I was curious to know why so many ignored its advice.

So there you have it. If you own no other books about investing, you should add these two to your personal library. You don't have to go far to buy books or seek advice on how to be bullish. These two will cement your ability to be skeptical as you keep yourself informed.

For those who plan to go further than these two, a warning and a few more recommendations. The warning: If you search Amazon for titles on the topic of "wealth management" or "ultra high net worth," the results will be littered with books on how to sell financial products to the wealthy as well as a great number of titles that simply re-hash disproved investment theories that have produced failure or, at best, mediocre results.

My recommendations: While not trying to create my own *New York Times* "must read" list, before buying the next book focusing on high net worth, here are a couple of titles aimed at the average investor from which you might benefit. *The Millionaire Next Door*, by Thomas J. Stanley, is at the top of the list. I am an advocate of Stanley's prose especially because of the way he discusses in such understandable language the importance of frugality, savings, and delaying gratification. As your appetite for knowledge increases, fortify your library with a copy of Howard Marks' *The Most Important Thing*. Marks, co-founder of Oaktree Capital Management, also shines in his conversational tone recounting the biggest inflection points of his career.

Targeted Reports Provide Unique Perspectives

If you wish to see what "the big money" is doing, there are a handful of annual surveys and online resources available for study:

You can find the *Yale University Endowment Report* at www.investments. yale.edu. While my previous writings and still current convictions caution investors about trying to mimic the investment habits of non-taxable endowments (because of the impact of portfolio taxes and the inability of most investors to access the same money managers), the endowment report offers the well-written perspective of one of the most successful institutional investors of our time, David Swensen. What I like most about the way the report is written is that the math pencils out. It gives the asset allocation for the entire portfolio, the expected return for the entire portfolio, and the expected return for each of the sub-asset classes within the portfolio. One might agree or disagree with its forward-looking assumptions (as being too bullish in the case of private equity); the reader will come away understanding an investment plan that has been well thought out. The *Yale University Endowment Report* does something else unique among its peers: it models a custom rate of inflation specific to the costs of education rather than following the CPI, a government attempt at measuring inflation across all parts of the economy. Good for Yale! This is important because the success of the endowment should allow the corpus to grow at a rate that will equal or exceed the cost of tuition at Yale, which has been growing faster than the CPI. If the fund was modeled on the CPI, and it grows at a rate of 3% annually but the cost of a college education grows 5%, fewer students would benefit from the fund or the corpus would be reduced. Instead, the fund is diligently modeled for outcomes based upon the needs of the ultimate constituents: future students.

The NACUBO survey, discussed in other chapters, is another online resource that communicates the performance and asset allocation of the largest US college endowments. You can view it at www.nacubo.org. For the same reasons, I repeat the warning I gave above about trying to put together a mirror image individual portfolio. Although the college endowment crowd was over-exposed to equity at the time of the 2000 peak and then to hedge funds over the next decade, NACUBO gives investors a window into how a massive amount of capital is invested. According to the 2018 NACUBO survey, the

809 participants in the survey held over a half trillion dollars in assets. Peering deeper into the report, you will discover that institutional investors struggle with the same issues as other investors: active versus passive, equity versus debt, traditional versus alternative, efficient versus inefficient markets, and so on. I am often asked the question, "How do I benchmark my entire portfolio against a peer group?" This survey is a start, and, as I have mentioned elsewhere in the book, knowing how one's portfolio has fared against the average US household, the average college endowment, and even the Forbes 400 gives enough data points to gauge success or failure according to your objectives.

Peer Groups Broaden Horizons

Once family assets exceed $50 million, many investors seek to engage in a national peer group to not only share knowledge and learn about investments, but to gain perspective on the softer issues of family governance, philanthropy, and estate planning.

IPI has the longest history as an educational and peer networking organization for substantial investors. I have been involved with IPI for over 17 years, having been appointed a family designate, which allows me to benefit from this group of families.

IPI was founded in 1991 by Charlotte Beyer, author of *Wealth Management Unwrapped*. Charlotte envisioned IPI as a way to narrow the gap between investors and advisors. What gap? The financial education gap, jargon gap, expectation gap, value proposition gap, expected return gap are but a few of the areas that Charlotte found needed improvement across the private investor landscape.

I came to know Charlotte in 2000, a year in which a few of my clients were involved in billion dollar liquidity events. Being 32 at the time, I was smart enough to know what I did not know. While I was proud of the investment success of the families for whom I worked, there were aspects of family governance, philanthropy, multigenerational estate planning where I knew I needed a deeper bench. One of my clients and I decided that we would join this organization together and use the occasion of their New York forums to learn from and to stimulate new ideas, which we would then vet in terms of their applicability to the work we were doing. I was very pleased with the results. Interacting with the members of IPI did exactly what I hoped it would, which was to widen my opportunity to interact with real families and other professionals managing large portfolios for a large number of beneficiaries, dull some of the personal bias that I had developed so that I could be more open to non-traditional investment tenets, and develop a network of family members, family office executives, and deep thinkers in the investment industry.

Charlotte had an amazing ability to ask great questions in her leadership role at the institute and when she interacted one on one with members. One such notable occasion for me happened in 2005 when she recommended that I attend the week-long Private Wealth Management course at the Wharton School of Business. The "Wharton program," as it is referred to by members, (discussed in Chap. 11) is held annually. The program, led by Professor Richard Marston and Ms. Beyer, extracts key components of the Certified Investment Management Analyst curriculum and reformulates the lessons to target families with high tax portfolios. At that time, there was a separate program for financial professionals and family office executives and another for family members; today, they are combined.

The days are filled with classroom lectures, working lunches and dinners, and evening study/small group discussions. Today, IPI is a subsidiary of Campden FB, a global organization that offers financial education conferences and networking opportunities. IPI's current president is Brien Biondi. One of its unique contributions to the private investor community is their annual Family Performance Tracking™ survey. Beginning in 2016, the Campden Global Family Office Report took over the role of reporting on individual family portfolio returns and asset allocations. In some years, the report lists portfolio allocations along with the net return earned in that specific year by asset class. Reading it, you will find families in which 100% of the portfolio is invested in hedge funds. On the opposite end of the spectrum, a handful of families have 90% or more of their portfolio allocated to high-grade municipal bonds.

Of particular interest to me (and I hope to you) is the average allocation to each asset class (global equity, domestic equity, high-grade municipal bonds, government bonds, junk bonds, private equity, venture capital, real estate, and hedge funds), which has borne a remarkable similarity to the allocations found in the NACUBO survey. Despite the fact that some high-tax families pay nearly 50% on each unit of short-term capital gains, taxable bonds, or hedge fund returns, their lack of attention to after-tax returns has caused them to suffer equal risk (compared to non-taxable institutional portfolios) while earning sub-par after-tax returns. Many investors belonging to IPI and Campden have increasingly been calling for Wall Street and the advisory community to report net returns to investors. Unfortunately, the call has not been loud enough to effect a change in the status quo. For now, private investors must choose between calculating after-tax returns themselves *and* limiting their investment choices to firms that are willing to report net returns. A Wall Street friend, addressing a group, said quite simply, "You cannot EAT gross returns."

Another organization that serves to educate and stimulate its members is TIGER 21, founded by Michael Sonnenfeldt. TIGER 21 differs materially from IPI in its scope and in the frequency of its meetings. TIGER stands for The Investment Group for Enhanced Results in the twenty-first century. They highlight that membership in the group creates a "personal board of directors" composed of the best minds in business. With 600 members, TIGER maintains that its members can claim personal assets exceeding $50 billion. I have addressed a TIGER meeting and found the group to include more "hands-on" investors than you might find among other investment networking groups. To gain admission to the group, your minimum net worth in personal assets must exceed $10 million. For obvious reasons members are concentrated around the New York and the Silicon Valley, but there are small groups who meet in over 25 cities.

A popular routine is what TIGER calls a "portfolio defense" session in which each investor shares the details of their portfolio. The member presenting will likely disclose the actual value of their portfolio, the allocation of assets, the outside managers and alternative investment vehicles employed, their historical performance, as well as the annual cash withdrawal they use to fund their living expenses. Members who attend these presentations are encouraged to ask pointed questions of the investor that might help them understand where bias has created a portfolio inconsistency, an unknown risk, or an opportunity that has not been deployed to its full potential. This unique process is highly valuable to members who are used to being told they are right by subordinates. A member who identifies their primary investment goal as preservation of capital, for example, might be grilled by other members if their portfolio was found to contain a high concentration of risky assets. Self-delusion is a cancer that infects many investors and the TIGER portfolio defense is surely a step in the right direction. Investors who wish to learn more should visit www.tiger21.com.

The Family Office Exchange (FOX) was founded by Sarah Hamilton in 1989. It is based in Chicago. The goal of FOX is to serve as a peer networking organization for families seeking an objective financial education about passing wealth successfully to future generations. Made up of family office executives, advisors, and private investors FOX boasts several pieces of industry research that thinned the veil on several aspects of the wealth management industry. In 1991, FOX released one of the first comprehensive studies on master custody costs for family office portfolios. In 1994, they published a study on family office compensation, structure, and benefits. Another benchmarking survey was released in 2008.

The leadership at FOX aims to adapt their research and survey content around the changing trends in the family office community. In 2011, FOX members were debating and questioning the effectiveness and validity of Modern Portfolio Theory and asked me to deliver an address, which I titled "Evaluating the Line-up of New Investment Approaches to Follow Modern Portfolio Theory." The research that led to that presentation ultimately fed into our work on the Efficient Valuation Hypothesis, addressed in Chap. 7.

I cannot reinforce enough the benefits to be gained from inserting yourself into an intellectually stimulating crucible of peers. It can produce results, ideas, and outcomes that would not be otherwise possible. I know from my own experience how valuable the call to learn from people with whom I disagree or perhaps misunderstand is. In fact, in my case, it is as strong today as it was back then when I was cutting my teeth as a young financial advisor.

Conclusion

I want to stress once more that finding a trusted advisor does not absolve you from educating yourself on the basics of portfolio allocation, money management, and the cause and effect relationships that lead to financial success. It is worth the time and financial commitment to strengthening your personal financial fluency.

Part III

Successful Spending, Philanthropy, Gifting and Estate Planning

14

Spending: How Much Is Too Much?

Let's not beat around the bush: the ultimate objective for every dollar a person has ever earned, invested, or saved is to get rid of it during their lifetime or by passing it on to heirs after their death. This is as certain as death and taxes. Whether you spend it, give it to charity, or leave it to heirs, it is a fact that it will leave your hands one way or another.

That said, spending money wisely in the here and now may be even more important than the charitable gifts you leave after you are gone. Dollars spent immediately compost (or redistribute, if you prefer that word) into the soil of the free market economy and into the hands of another consumer. For that reason, I have actually advised clients, for whom giving was not a priority, to ask themselves the following question: if I had $1000 and I had the opportunity to leave an extra $50 tip for the waitress at each of my next 20 meals *or* to randomly give out $50 bills in a poor neighborhood from the back of a truck, which would accomplish the greater good? Certainly, both exhibit benevolence, but does one have a more lasting effect on the recipient than the other? The $50 tip may have a cause and effect relationship that promotes better service in the future; both acts could have a copycat effect where other customers or passersby (observing your generosity) decide to do the same, further composting the wealth. It is not an easy question to answer.

A purposeful, deliberate spending policy is the quickest and most efficient way for you to accomplish the inevitable redistribution of your wealth. It can also be an incredibly enjoyable experience once you decide on this course of wealth management. It may come as a surprise to you, but I have had to counsel more clients about spending more money than I have had to counsel them

© The Author(s) 2019
N. J. Gannon, *Tailored Wealth Management*,
https://doi.org/10.1007/978-3-319-99780-3_14

about curtailing or reducing spending. Yet this should not come as a surprise since the most successful wealthy families got that way through saving, shrewd investing, and delaying gratification.

Pinpointing the day you decide to begin to reward yourself can easily fall victim to procrastination. A small percentage of families consciously decide to create a Franciscan wealth distribution plan. That is, that they decide to give 90% or more of their wealth to charity during their lifetimes or at their death. One member of the St. Louis community did just that. E. Desmond Lee sold his company, Lee Rowan Corporation, for approximately $75 million in 1993. Over the next two decades, Lee managed to award $70 million in grants to a variety of benevolent organizations in the St. Louis region.[1] Lee was justly praised for his selfless distribution of wealth. While spending $70 million won't earn you the same headline in your obituary than if you gave it away, you will have still moved those dollars from your bank account into someone else's.

Regardless of how you decide to spend your wealth, it is important to strike the right spending policy because once you establish a budget, it is important you spend it on your intended purposes. If you have done well and have a large portfolio, your spending is important both to your family and to the community at large. I will discuss the importance of philanthropy in Chap. 15, but, on this point I am certain, the quickest and most effective way to compost your wealth is to spend it wisely.

My friend Laurie Phillips, CEO of the St. Patrick's Center for the Homeless in St. Louis, gave me her more informed perspective on this topic. She used the example of encountering two homeless people on the street: one asks you for $10 for dinner and bus fare; the other asks you for $10 for a picture he painted on a piece of driftwood. The money each receives is the same, but in the latter case, you have received something in return. As Laurie explained, that item may provoke deep thoughts or more compassion for people living on the street. You have engaged in a free market transaction where you have gotten something for your money, but you have also complimented the man on his work, and have sent him a message that he can do it again. Furthermore, Laurie says, you have sent an even stronger message to the first man, who witnessed the whole thing: perhaps he isn't able to paint, but maybe it will lead him to consider what he can do.

Phillips also suggests something else you might do instead of just handing him $10; for example, you might drive him to the homeless shelter or call him an Uber and instruct the driver to take him to the homeless shelter. Most

---

[1] St. Louis Post-Dispatch, "He Gave $70 Million to Schools, Arts here," January 13, 2010.

certainly, spending the $10 on something the homeless man is selling or helping the first man get help is more likely to help him than dropping money into his cup and walking away. This is not to diminish the biblical principle of doing good for others while expecting nothing in return.

The broader point I am trying to establish here is that even if you drop a dollar into the case of a man playing the saxophone (even if he isn't exactly playing like Kenny G), the process of spending in exchange for some good or service repeats itself around the world millions of time each day. Think for a moment about the money you spend in a year and what happens when those dollars transfer out of your account into the accounts of chefs, waiters, violinists, florists, housekeepers, mechanics, carpenters, and landscape architects. Every time you spend $1 on one of these professionals' services, you are engaging in a transaction similar to giving $10 to the homeless artist or the street musician. You are getting something in return, you are complimenting the professional for their work, and both of you are hoping the transaction recurs multiple times in the future.

To Spend or Not to Spend

Americans have fallen in love with the tale of the humble billionaire who lives in a modest house, drives a ten-year-old pickup truck, and, on his death, leaves all his money to charity. While this folksy tale sounds altruistic, the billionaire loves sitting on his pile of cash and, while he wags his finger at you for owning a Prada purse or drinking a nice glass of Veuve Clicquot, his cash will not benefit society for many decades until his death.

The difference between the frugal billionaire and Ron Reade (see Chap. 2) is striking. The frugal billionaire loves the public image he has created and feeds it with press appearances and photo shoots in money magazines. Mr. Reade (who seemed to spend very little money) did not seek to create an image for himself. A billionaire who spends 5% of his wealth each year will have redistributed all of the original $1 billion over 20 years. Sure, he hopes that his portfolio will generate an investment return that will replace the dollars spent, but that spending is the surest thing that he and his employees, vendors, and bartenders can count on. In this chapter, I will attempt to provide some perspective on my own journey and the journeys I've witnessed of clients and friends.

The financial planning industry seems to focus on an average spending policy of around 4% of assets. In theory, this is intended to allow assets to grow at a rate that will allow an inflation hedge on the principle of the portfolio

NET of annual withdrawals. Earlier, in discussing investing, I cautioned against relying too much on rigid historically based rules, mainly because applying such rules rests on achieving historical asset class performance. At the time of this writing (early 2018), rates of return on short-term bank deposits, certificates of deposits, and intermediate bonds are well below historical averages. Thus, a 4% spending policy may be too high, especially for the investor who insists on a fixed income dominant allocation and for whom growth of capital is a priority.

Decisions: When to Spend It, What to Spend It On

The wealth trait that I believe you should acquire is *flexibility*. In the same way the business you built—the source of your wealth—had to be flexible to compete, so too must your new "business" of spending be. Think about the decisions you made in the early days of your business. At times, you had to cut back to only the essentials. There were times when you had to rev the engines at full tilt to gain an advantage in the market. As a consumer or spender, you should remind yourself that flexibility is not something to fear. It is what brought your business from point A to point B.

By flexibility I mean the ability to change. One example would be a flexible budget, so that if you decided to cut back, you could still maintain spending on specific parts of it. For example, a family with a $1 million budget (net of taxes) should be able to split that spending up in whatever way they wish (assuming they haven't acquired too many toys and bricks on borrowed money). Such a family might spend their money this way:

- $100,000 tithe to the family's favorite charities
- $300,000 for 50 hours on a light jet fractional program for personal travel
- $200,000 spent on general leisure travel with friends and family
- $200,000 on maintenance of personal residence(s)
- $200,000 on food, clothing, restaurants, and entertainment

This budget offers a massive amount of flexibility. Think for a second how you would spend your money if you had a million dollar budget. I can imagine my readers looking at that budget and immediately polarizing on the subject of private air travel. Some will say that the cost is so astronomical compared to the benefit, they would rather spend the money on something else. Others, and believe me I have heard this very thing, would rather eat beans and toast and shop at Old Navy than give up their private air travel. Fair enough. Those that don't mind the overnight dry mouth and extra day of fatigue after an overseas trip will immediately have $250,000 to spend on something else (let's assume this family flies business class or premium economy). Others will look at the cost of the personal and vacation residences and either expand or contract that part of their budget based upon the amount of time they use the property. Some families give zero to charity, while others prefer to give 20%, even 30%, of their budget to this slice of the pie. The point is that when people are truly wealthy, they will not look at the budget and wring their hands over possibly losing the ability to fly private. If it's important to them, they will just cut somewhere else and prioritize one item over another.

Near the trough of the 2009 financial crisis I remember having a conversation with a client who was worried about the decline in stock market prices and felt the need to "cut back." While it took some strong coaxing, I convinced the client that there was no reason to do that. His portfolio had declined by only a fraction of the downturn that higher-risk portfolios had. One hundred percent of the cash flow he needed for his yearly expenses was covered by the cash flow from his dividends and bond interest, which meant the market value of his portfolio was immaterial to his spending. Finally, I asked whether he personally felt that he should do his part in extending the recession by canceling vacations, restaurant reservations, and laying off household staff *or* if he should take the role of an adaptable business owner and support the very businesses that needed his patronage now more than ever. Remember, for a hotel or restaurant going from 100% occupancy to 80% can spell the end. If certain restaurants or vacation resorts are important to a family, should they not continue to patronize them so they have a chance of staying in business?

In the end, this client, who was shrewd in his investment posture leading into and during the crisis and who had been zealously charitable for decades, agreed that he had earned the right to enjoy himself in 2009 and 2010 regardless of what his investments looked like on paper, and decided to give meaningful amounts of his net worth to members of his extended family. His decisions strengthened my belief that he was wealthy.

The takeaway: If you fly private, eight to ten of the seats on your plane will be for your guests whether they are friends or family. Most of the wine in that special bottle will pour into a glass other than your own. I say this to illustrate the point that even when you are spending money on the finer things in life, you are sharing your good fortune with others. If you have become successful enough to enjoy the privilege of these jewels, enjoy them but never let them own you. If you can do that, you can also stave off or put off the day when they may bore you. And if or when that day comes, be flexible enough to do something else for yourself, your family, or your community.

Of course, my client has his polar opposite, sadly. His alter-ego would likely go into the crisis over-exposed because he was always looking for "more." A 50% drop in the stock market in 2009 led many family portfolios (as evidenced by industry surveys) to lose 30% or more of their total value (as private equity and other assets also under-performed expectations). This person cannot imagine a world where he couldn't have it all. He MUST fly private. He MUST stay in the finest five-star resorts around the world. He MUST drink only the finest wines from every region, and his palate is satisfied by only the trendiest award-winning chefs. When crisis hits, he usually experiences every Richter scale reading of the financial quake, and immediately frets about what to do next.

The takeaway: The man who MUST have everything is not wealthy, he is not flexible, and for him, the stress of the crisis most certainly is not conducive to enjoying life. While I have known and met people who fall into this camp, I have been fortunate enough never to have worked for them.

The Joy of Spending

If you have planned well for your heirs and your favorite charities, it's time to enjoy the rest of your portfolio. Sharpen your mettle like a warrior who is prepared for anything the financial markets could send your way, then take a big breath of life and smell the roses. You made the money; you've earned its fruits.

Clients often look around in the last few decades of life and believe they have too much "stuff." That Waterford Crystal ship decanter that looked like such a good deal at the duty-free store in the Dublin airport now fails to evoke emotion or memory of that first trip to Ireland. The wine cellar is declared to be "too full to be consumed in my lifetime." Artisan furniture that you thought would become a family heirloom doesn't meet the decorating taste of your children. In the end, a phone call to a local charity is made, and the aging collector "molts" his old skin and adapts to a simpler, less cluttered life ahead.

In observing families who have lived well, I rarely hear them talk with regret about a trip they took with their family or extended family. Experiences tend to grow finer and evoke more joy as time progresses whereas things often degrade or lose their glow. One family with young children took their grandmother on a fabulous Alaskan cruise when she was in her mid-80s. They purchased three adjoining cabins, each with balconies where they could marvel at the beauty of the orcas or the calving glaciers. As the grandchildren grew older, they learned from their parents that their grandmother had visited 49 of the 50 states and they wanted to give her the gift of seeing the fiftieth. The message to the youngsters was less about the luxury of a boutique Alaskan cruise and more about doing something nice for grandma.

Another family has a great tradition with their grandchildren. The year in which the grandchild turns 16, this family of practicing Catholics, take the grandchild on a pilgrimage to Rome. Over a few special dinners and tours in the Eternal City, the grandparents have the unique opportunity of communicating their pride in the youngster, their optimism that the child will find success, and to share a story or two about what success meant in their own life. They are able to tell the story about why they tithe to international charities that aim to lighten the burden of life in the developing world. This may not motivate a sluggish teenager or guarantee that they will practice the faith in which they were raised, tithe money to charity, or work at the family business, but it is guaranteed to give the grandparents the gift of time with their grandchildren. The grandchildren gain a memory of that time when grandma and grandpa bought them gelato after every meal, when they were given the opportunity to view Rome from the cupola of St. Peters, and the vivid memory of hearing their grandparent say, "I'm proud of you."

A very good friend takes his extended family on a Caribbean or other warm weather vacation every year after Christmas. A handful of his family members don't appreciate this gift. They think their brother-in-law has money to burn. To my friend, this doesn't matter. He isn't looking for credit. He is genuinely grateful that life has been good to him and that he has the ability to give this gift to his family.

Very early in my career there was a financial adviser who had formerly practiced as a CPA. In addition to advising her widowed client on her portfolio, her tasks grew over time to include bookkeeping, bill paying, and performing other administrative tasks. The two had a mostly social lunch date scheduled every Wednesday. The advisor was proud of the work she did for her client and believed that no one knew more about her client's affairs. When the client passed away, the advisor received a call from the client's attorney who requested a meeting. The advisor shared with the attorney, "that won't be necessary. I have a copy of her will and trust here in the office and will be prepared to distribute the estate as you direct." The attorney replied, "You do not know everything. What you have isn't the most current copy of the estate plan." The advisor agreed to meet with the attorney, at which time he communicated that the entire estate was to go to her. The client and her children had regrettably become estranged and hadn't spoken once in the last 20 years of her life. To her, her advisor had become family and the decision to make her the beneficiary had been made over a decade before she died. The advisor, then in her early 40s, decided to retire, moved to Hawaii with her spouse, and adopted a baby.

When Spending Goes Wrong

In the late 1990s, ousted Tyco CEO Dennis Kozlowski became the poster boy for lavish corporate excess. Kozlowski and the board of directors who approved his pay package received one of the most notable pay packages on Wall Street. Shortly before accounting irregularities, fraud, and other charges were brought against Kozlowski and his fellow executives, Kozlowski, who loved to party, threw a party—a very big party. The venue was the island of Sardinia off the coast of Italy. Who's Who celebrities were on hand. Headliner bands played. Lavish food and wine were served. Nothing would be imprinted on the minds of guests more than the most notable guest of all. His name was David, a 15-foot-tall ice sculpture replica of Michelangelo's masterpiece. Unlike the original, this David's penis spouted vodka. All you could drink. Tyco crashed; Kozlowski eventually went to jail.

Still, there is some good news. Guess who kept the money spent on that Sardinian bash? It was the waiters, bartenders, musicians, florists, ice sculptors, chauffeurs, innkeepers, airline crews, and anyone else who made their living from the venue's luxury business.

The takeaway: In addition to wanting to evoke a smile, I wanted to remind you that even conspicuous consumption has a rapid distributive impact on the economy.

Conclusion

A well-thought-out spending plan recognizes that we are only temporary owners of wealth. Experiences tend to improve with time, material things tend to diminish, to become less important. Spend your wealth wisely, in a manner that does not deplete the well too quickly, and enjoy it. That is what you worked for all of those years.

15

Philanthropy: What You Need to Know to Donate Wisely

If done effectively and deliberately, giving money away can give you one of the strongest adrenaline rushes available to a human being. A philanthropic dollar can also give you one of the largest, if not the largest, returns on investment available. (I'll cover the arithmetic of this later in this chapter.) The purpose of this chapter is to provide you with a 50,000-foot-view of the state of American giving so that you can make an informed decision as to how you will participate, or if you wish to participate at all.

The 2017 Giving USA report produced by the Indiana University Lilly Family School of Philanthropy reported that Americans gave $390 billion to philanthropic causes in the previous year.[1] As Fig. 15.1 illustrates, by donor category, individuals contributed 15 times more than corporations.

Of the $390 billion, $281 billion was contributed by individuals. The next largest donor class, foundations, contributed $59 billion. It should be noted that a significant number of foundations trace their funding back to gifts from individuals. Another $30 billion was contributed by individuals through bequests by way of their wills or trusts. The smallest donor category was corporations at $18.5 billion. Combining individual contributions across the sub-categories inclusive of outright gifts, gifts at death, and gifts through family foundations, individual gifts eclipsed corporate gifts by twenty to one. Americans, as measured by the dollars they give, are indeed generous.

---

[1] Giving USA: The Annual Report on Philanthropy for the Year 2016 (2017). Chicago: Giving USA Foundation™.

© The Author(s) 2019
N. J. Gannon, *Tailored Wealth Management*,
https://doi.org/10.1007/978-3-319-99780-3_15

DONOR TYPE (IN BILLIONS $)

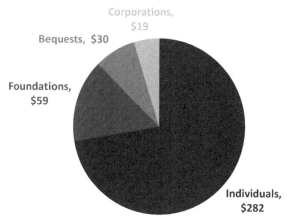

Corporations, $19

Bequests, $30

Foundations, $59

Individuals, $282

Fig. 15.1 Donor type in billions

As you will see, a tax-deductible philanthropic gift gives the donor who is looking for the maximum bang for her buck tremendous leverage.

Donations to Religious Organizations

The largest recipient category of American giving is to religious organizations. At $122 billion, it represents 31% of all donations. There are differing views on the subject of giving about whether giving to one's own church or faith group is a philanthropic or self-serving act. A June 23, 2014, blog post on Forbes.com highlighted a quote from billionaire and once US presidential candidate Jon Huntsman about his personal view of giving to his church. The author of the blog, Andrew Cave, noted that Huntsman had already given $1.5 billion representing 80% of his net worth to worthy causes. But on the topic of giving through the church collection basket, Huntsman said:

> My philanthropy is not borne out of my faith. They require 10% tithing. I don't consider that to be philanthropy and I don't consider it to be part of my philanthropic giving. I consider it as club dues.
>
> People who put money in the church basket and people who go to church and pay the pastor: that isn't real philanthropy, that's just like you belong to a country club. You pay your dues to belong to that church so you pay your tithing or whatever it is. I've never added that into my philanthropy in any way because I just think it's a part of a person's life.

Huntsman's point is that true philanthropy is giving to a cause where we are not a stakeholder or a beneficiary of the cause, even if in a small way. The donor category statistics in the Giving USA report reflect this belief; 70% of all donations go to something other than religion or religious causes. Unlike Mr. Huntsman, I doubt that all donations directed at religious causes fall into the "country club" dues category. Many religious organizations engage in work that directly helps the poor, aids the homeless, delivers healthcare services, and provides disaster relief. Indeed, many of the most effective human service organizations were born out of or continue to be efficiently and effectively administered by a church or religious group.

Donations to Other Organizations

The Giving USA 2017 Report, illustrated in Fig. 15.2, breaks the beneficiaries down for us:

- $122 billion to religion
- $60 billion to education
- $47 billion to human services

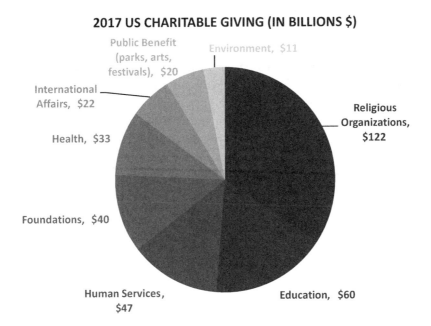

2017 US CHARITABLE GIVING (IN BILLIONS $)

Fig. 15.2 Donation beneficiaries

- $40 billion to foundations (who then likely donate across all categories)
- $33 billion to health
- $22 billion to international affairs (including for relief of non-US poverty)
- $20 billion to public society benefit (parks, festivals, civic events, etc.)
- $11 billion to environment and animals

Nationally, while the dollars seem large, Americans donate, on average, 3 to 4% of their income. Some contribute nothing, while others contribute 10 to 50% of their annual income. In my practice as an advisor, one-third of my clients display a deep personal commitment to giving. I have seen large gifts to fund family foundations coincident with the sale of their family business. Among those who are working, I have observed a few families who annually give 20%, even 30%, of pre-tax income to a variety of causes. For these families, giving is deeply personal, and this is reflected throughout American giving as reflected in the Indiana University report.

Enlightened Giving

Just as wealth creators will want to be wise stewards of where they spend their money, informed philanthropists will want to be equally wise stewards of the dollars they give away. Giving, at the beginning, is generally born more out of emotion than reason. As donors mature and begin to allocate more to philanthropy, the more deliberate and refined they are in their attitude toward giving.

One family we advise developed a personal philanthropy campaign after the devastation of the 2017 hurricane season in the eastern Caribbean Islands. As frequent visitors aboard the family's yacht to these countries, seeing the destruction caused by hurricanes Irma and Maria prompted a call to action. Phone calls to the islands assured them that while there was no loss of life among the many vendors with whom they had done business, the tourism industry, upon which most families relied, was shattered and that it was estimated to take years for the islands to recover.

On the island of St. Thomas, US Virgin Islands, the family was connected with Bishop Herbert Bevard, who began a campaign to open the Catholic schools on St. Thomas, St. John, and St. Croix to all students regardless of their ability to pay tuition. The bishop had observed that in the aftermath of past storms some public schools closed because their teachers returned to the mainland, leaving a gap in the various communities. The family decided that they would contribute $100,000 to this effort, an amount roughly equal to what they would have spent in the local economy had the storm not occurred. Subsequently, the family became aware of the BVI Unite campaign, spearheaded by the British Virgin Islands' most famous resident, Sir Richard Branson of Virgin Atlantic. Since Sir Richard pledged to cover 100% of the operating costs of this philanthropic effort, the family made another grant of $100,000 to rebuild one of the schools on the island of Tortola. This family, who witnessed the devastation of the storm on television, asked themselves, "If we don't help these people, who will?"

The Joy of Giving

To my young readers, I say, begin early. Giving 10% of your salary may sound like a lot if you are making $25,000 per year. Start with 3 or 4% (the national average), then grow into making a larger percentage gift as your salary grows. Just as I urge young people to begin their careers with a robust savings rate of 15% and then growing it to 25% or more, I believe the same habits can be honed early and then refined as time passes. If you begin saving AND giving before you have painted yourself into the corner of large rent and car payments, your journey will be easier. I have NEVER met a person who regrets giving money away. Never.

Jon Huntsman began giving at an early age, and it is clear from reading transcripts of his speeches and interviews that he feels a personal euphoria from the act of giving:

> As a young man, I was a navy officer in Vietnam. I made $320 a month and would always give away $50 a month to a family I felt that was in greater need than me, in addition to my tithing to my church. I've just always felt in my heart, coming from a very humble background, that there are plenty of people who need a break in life. As a senior in high school with no money working several jobs, I was sent to a great school on the east coast by a wonderful Jewish man. I've never forgotten that. I've sent over 5,000 young people to school around the world in memory of him because he was so gracious to me. It's been very easy in my heart to give money back and help causes that are meritorious.

One of my favorite stories of giving was recounted to me by a friend who volunteered to collect funds for a charity fundraiser for the homeless after Mass the Saint Louis Basilica. A woman in tattered clothes, elderly and slouched, approached the desk with a pledge card in her hand. Paper clipped to the pledge card was one dollar and one quarter. My friend looked at the card and saw the woman had pledged $5, and checked that she would pay it in quarterly in installments. Can we really say that we don't have the capacity to give when stories like this are not uncommon across our neighborhoods and communities? I know that this woman's act caused my friend to make a larger donation than she intended, and who knows what compounding effect that woman's initial act had on others who heard about it?

The poorest in our society might logically have earned a pass on the duty to help others, but in many cases they step up to the plate. The volunteers who worked the pledge drive that evening believe that woman probably made the largest gift as a percentage of discretionary income of anyone in attendance.

The Value of Giving

Is there a "value" to giving? I believe there is and I'm not only speaking about the euphoria that comes from helping others. There is a definite economic value in giving money away, especially in view of the advantages afforded to philanthropic gifts in the US tax code.

First, let's dispel the myth that a donor somehow gets something back when she gives away a dollar. The "write off" myth is just that, a myth. The tax code does indeed allow donors to exclude philanthropic dollars from their adjusted gross income because these dollars no longer are an asset of the donor. Simply put, the charitable deduction allows a person who earns $2 and keeps $1 for himself and gives away $1 to a philanthropic cause to owe tax only on the $1 that remains.

In terms of value, however, I submit to you that $1 given away to a qualified charitable cause is worth 100% more than a dollar kept for oneself net of taxes paid. Let me explain. Suppose that the person is in the 37% tax bracket and lives in the state of California where she pays an additional 13.3% in state taxes. In the first scenario, the worker decides to keep $1 of every $2 she makes. For the first dollar, she must subtract 37 cents for federal tax and another 13.3% for California tax. What is left of the first dollar is 50 cents.

On the dollar she donates directly to a qualified charity that is excluded from her adjusted gross income, no tax is due. Once the charity receives the dollar, they are free to spend it directly on the programs organic to their mission. The dollar allocated, let's say, to earthquake relief remains $1 as opposed to the dollar retained by worker, which was reduced to 50 cents. The gifted dollar is thus worth 100% more in economic benefit than the dollar retained for personal consumption.

This exercise is addressed to the family whose cup runneth over, not to those who are struggling to pay for the basics of life. I simply wish to stress that once we have adequately funded the things that we need for our own families that we can have double the economic effect once we decide to help a stranger's family.

Tailored Philanthropy for the Wealthy Family

The most economically beneficial time to build your family foundation or donor-advised fund is coincident with the sale of the family business. Many of America's largest family foundations and funds were financed at the liquidation of the business OR at the death of the founder. In this section, we'll look at a few examples of each, those that succeeded as well as a few public instances where well-intended philanthropy either failed completely or failed to fulfill its potential.

In *Investing Strategies*, I noted the example of Dennis and Judy Jones of St. Louis, Missouri, who chose to tithe 10% of the gross sales proceeds of their stake in Jones Pharma into the Dennis M Jones Family Foundation, which focuses on education and social services. The gift occurred in the fourth quarter of 2000, and Dennis was proud that the foundation received the highest selling price for a share of stock than even members of his family. On one million shares of stock, the foundation received roughly $52 million. Since that day, the foundation has distributed over $40 million in gifts to charitable organizations at the same time as it has grown the corpus.

Coincident with the creation of the Jones Foundation, I am aware of at least six other families who used the proceeds of their ownership stake in Jones Pharma to fund a family foundation or other philanthropic project. Some of these families are intensely private, wishing to quietly fund projects and refrain from appearing in the public eye. Others believe that it is important for peers to learn from one another and to entice others to act by first setting the example. The decision to be public or private in one's philanthropy must be discerned by each individual family as a reflection of their goals and priorities. There is no right or wrong answer on the point of anonymous versus public philanthropy.

Protect Yourself from Giving Going Awry

Can philanthropy take a detour or deviate fully from the intent of the wealth creator? It certainly can. In 2012, the *Wall Street Journal* published a story titled "When Philanthropy Goes Wrong" citing cases of the foundations seeded by Henry Ford, oil magnate Howard Pew, and other twentieth-century tycoons where the ultimate activities and grants were in direct opposition to the causes espoused by their founders. The authors rightly assigned partial blame to the founders themselves for not leaving specific instructions, and even prohibitions to those to whom the foundations legacy was entrusted.

A new trend has developed in the shadow of cases such as the Ford and Pew foundations where founding members of a family foundation sunset the life of the foundation after a finite number of years. Sunset clauses seek to put the money to work over a finite number of years as opposed to creating an entity that could conceivably go on in perpetuity opening up the possibility that the corpus of the funds will never be spent on philanthropic causes the wealth creator intended.

Foundations like the Gates and Buffett foundations, funded by the wealth of two of the wealthiest people in the world, could have an outsized impact in proportion to donations or funding from individuals, governments, and even corporations. According to the Gates Foundation website, it has made $41.3 billion in cumulative grants since inception. While this amount is not enough to eclipse the $16.8 billion awarded globally through USAID in 2017, one could reasonably say that the Gates Foundation's giving power has already eclipsed the GDP of many countries.

In 2011, the *St. Louis Business Journal* ran a story titled "The End of the Danforth Foundation." The story marked the foundation's final gift of $70 million to the Donald Danforth Plant Science Center dedicated to the mission of improving the human condition through plant science. The Danforth Foundation had been established by William H. Danforth some 80 years prior to the final gift. Over its life, the foundation distributed more than $1.2 billion to various philanthropic organizations. Former US Senator John "Jack" Danforth was kind enough to speak to me about his memory of his grandfather and the thinking behind closing the foundation. "It was time," he said. At the fourth and now fifth generations of the family, the descendants of his grandfather numbered over 50. It seemed appropriate to "compost" the remaining capital into a younger, more contemporary organization that had focus, energy, and vigor. The family seemed to be very much at peace to be able to pass the torch in this way.

Focus of Giving: Determining Your Purpose

Susan Remmer Ryczewic's father and mother sold their family business in 1989. The Remmer Family Foundation was established in 1991. Her parents were the first generation of their family to go to college and both received merit-based scholarships to do so. Susan recalls, "My father was about business and family. It was those two things and those two things only. He was very utilitarian."

At the sale of the family business and the establishment of the foundation as their legacy, the Remmers created a family mission statement: "Reduce poverty for women and youth by helping disadvantaged adolescent and pre-adolescent girls take ownership of their lives. Create a level playing field through innovative programs in education, training and support. Encourage environmental stewardship with a focus on improving the sustainability of the world's fisheries."

Mr. Remmer was only 64 when he passed away, but his vision of inclusiveness and continuity paid dividends. For Susan's mother, Patricia, a core tenet of the foundation had to focus on opportunities for girls. She also wanted to ensure that as time passed and subsequent generations multiplied the foundation was to remain focused on its core principles and that it would not become a pass-through for the personal interests of succeeding generations; the family now numbers 34 descendants. Mrs. Remmer believed that while it was her role to set an example of giving and service, Susan recalled her as saying, "You cannot MAKE people do things."

When I speak to clients on topics such as this, I ask them to envision two scenarios which I have over-simplified here in order to make a point. Let's assume you have a choice between funding two projects. One project (costing $1 million) will fill helicopters with bags of rice that will be expeditiously dropped into communities suffering from a devastating famine. In this scenario, the objective is to maximize the number of lives saved. In the second scenario, you have an opportunity to purchase a rice plantation on behalf of a community for $1 million. Here, you are able to purchase the plantation from a for-profit corporation and gift it to the community, thereby allowing them to become subsistence farmers and feed their families for many years. Which one do you pick? If you select the latter, you will have selected the choice that is likely to be sustainable over many years, but it will save fewer lives than the former where saving the maximum number of lives is a priority.

It's not an easy decision. If you are doing your end-of-year online gifting, you might click the "donate $1000" to fund a project such as a community drinking water well or the purchase of a milking cow. However, the deeper you delve into the cause and effect relationship of your role in this ecosystem, the more you will question whether you are prudently spending (or investing) those funds.

Altruistic Giving Through Non-Traditional Channels

Most research on philanthropy studies the charitable giving reported by individuals and corporations on their tax returns. There are other sources of giving that cannot be measured through tax filings and some of them are new in the world of philanthropy.

Www.gofundme.com has become a popular way for anyone to start a fundraising campaign. While many of the projects one sees on these popular crowdfunding sites aim to raise money for projects that might be funded by a traditional non-profit corporation, they differ in one material way: the donors do NOT get a tax deduction for their contribution. Indeed, frivolous campaigns that aim to help a teenager take a vacation to Hawaii may occasionally show up on the site, but there also are many notable and sensible causes that donors can search on any given day. On the day of this writing, one of the campaigns on the front page of the site was started by a group of neighbors who were raising money for a family who lost their home in a fire.

In my home community of St. Louis, a www.gofundme.com campaign highlighted community altruism in a special way by bringing a special needs man named Raynard Nebbitt back to his home neighborhood.[2] Raynard's is a well-known face in the community of Webster Groves. For several decades, he rode his bicycle to a bridge overpass of Interstate 44 and signaled to trucks to blow their horns. He stayed for hours; basking in this repetitive exercise brought happiness in a way understood only by him. On his ride to and from the bridge, onlookers could clearly see that a model of the bridge (which Raynard built) was carefully balanced on the handlebars of his bike. In October of 2015, his sister Kathy was diagnosed with a skin disease and subsequently lost her job and their home. They were forced to move to a cheaper neighborhood in the city of St. Louis, but that didn't stop Raynard from visiting his beloved bridge, although his daily commute on his bike increased to two hours. Neighbors who learned of the family's difficulties stepped in with a crowdfunding campaign and raised $34,000 by Thanksgiving of 2017. This was enough to allow the Nebbitt's to rent a two-bedroom apartment in Webster

---

[2] St. Louis Post-Dispatch, "Raynard Nebbitt, a fixture on a bridge over I-44 for 20 years, returns home to Webster Groves," January 20, 2018.

and bring Reynard closer to where he called "home." Nobody in the Webster community received a tax deduction for their contribution. Many gave to the campaign anonymously. There were no black-tie galas where photographs of the donors looking dapper might show up in the society pages of the newspaper. This was a campaign focused solely on Raynard and his sister. Whether it counts as philanthropy in the eyes of the Internal Revenue Service matters not. Good people came together to help a neighbor for no other reason than that. Seek out stories like this in your own community. The next time you catch yourself questioning whether philanthropy has a role to play in our society, see if reading a story like this inspires you to do something new.

When it comes to giving, it is a decision which cannot be made with a slide rule or a calculator alone. The objective is to remove one's biases, discern the REAL reason behind the act of giving, and consider the cause and effect relationship between action and inaction, then march forward with the plan. For those who have not developed a systematized plan, there is always time to start. Your first gift will likely be an emotional one: a gift to alleviate a famine, hurricane, or earthquake relief or an extra generous slip of a $100 bill into the Salvation Army kettle outside of your grocery store. If you are one of the many who is called, capable, and generous enough to move the needle in our society, you'll know it in the core of your being. After that, it will be impossible for you not to act.

A Word of Warning

In recent years, philanthropists including those who have pledged to give away half or more of their wealth have been criticized for trying to "play God" or to disguise their desire for authoritarian control as global philanthropy. Despite being one of the most vocal advocates for those suffering from poverty, U2 lead singer Bono has been criticized for "stealing the voice" of Africa. The Bill and Melinda Gates Foundation has also endured its share of critics who second guess how they prioritize their projects, which range from anti-malaria mosquito nets to clean drinking water programs. From my perspective, I tip my hat to Bono and to Mr. Gates who chose to do something rather than do nothing. Saint Mother Teresa was sage in her advice to those who are criticized for trying to positively impact the world through philanthropy. A prayer attributed to her is painted on the wall of her home for children in Kolkata, India. It goes as follows:

People are often unreasonable, irrational, and self-centered. Forgive them anyway. If you are kind, people may accuse you of selfish ulterior motives. Be kind anyway. If you are successful, you will win some unfaithful friends and some genuine enemies. Succeed anyway. If you are honest and sincere people may deceive you. Be honest and sincere anyway. What you spend years creating, others could destroy overnight. Create anyway. If you find serenity and happiness, some may be jealous. Be happy anyway. The good you do today, will often be forgotten. Do good anyway. Give the best you have, and it will never be enough. Give your best anyway. In the final analysis, it is between you and God. It was never between you and them anyway.

The "Given Pledge": How You Can Give Like a Billionaire

Earlier in this chapter, I mentioned the Giving Pledge, a club reserved for billionaires (or those who can prove that they would have been billionaires had it not been for their philanthropy) who pledge to give 50% or more of their total net worth to charity during their life or at death. Those who take the pledge do so publicly and as of June 2018, the group boasts $365 billion in philanthropic dollars pledged.

I am calling for a new coalition to take a different pledge: the Given Pledge. The Given Pledge has the ability to eclipse the giving of the billionaire group if those who take it stick to a simple principle: tithing.

Most sacred texts of the major Abrahamic religions (Jewish, Christian, and Muslim) have a version of the 10% tithe of the faithful for the common good. Even some agnostic societies of secular humanists practice the tithe in some form or other. Many who practice the tithe also feel called to give in a subtle or private way so that they themselves will receive no societal benefit as a result. The group that elects to simply practice the tithe will make up the Given Pledge. The group will differ from the billionaires *Giving* Pledge in the following ways:

- Its focus as the word GIVEN implies is on what happens AFTER the funds have been put to work in a philanthropic purpose. As I see it, the focus word GIVING is on the donor; the idea of getting those of great wealth to *give* it away.
- Its membership will not be public. The pledge and the accountability for adhering to it will be policed by the person you see in the mirror in the morning.
- Members will orally pass down this value to family members.
- Members will practice a 10% tithe on pre-tax gross income during their lifetime, and will pledge another 10% tithe from their estate at the time of their death.

- Like the members of the billionaire Giving Pledge, the members of the Given Pledge will have donated a cumulative amount over their lifetime equal to or greater than half of their peak net worth.

In America today, with a population of roughly 300 million, we can assume that there are 100 million households. If just 1% of households (one million in all) take the pledge, the group will achieve a lifetime commitment to philanthropy that exceeds the wealth pledged by members of the billionaire Giving Pledge. Here is how the arithmetic works:

- One million households with an average of $54,000 in pre-tax income would donate an average of $5400 in year one. Assuming that their wage growth (and subsequent donations grow at a rate of 3% per year), over four decades they will have donated $407,000 (on average) per family. Assuming one million members (1% of American households), this brings the cumulative lifetime giving of the group to $407 billion.
- Let's assume that this household also begins saving with the same diligence as their giving; that is, they contribute a minimum of 15% of their pre-tax wages to their qualified retirement plan every year and let's assume the same 3% rate of annual inflation on their contributions, that would put this family at a cumulative savings of $1,179,000 by the time they reach 65. Even without considering appreciation or taking investment return into account, clearly the couple could expect to amass a larger nest egg over time, and 10% of that nest egg tithed at death comes to $117,900 per family or $117,900,000,000! (Clearly they'd need to withdraw something from their nest egg for continued living expenses; more on that a little later.)

How powerful is it that if 1% of American households would decide to live the spirit of the scriptural tithe required by their Bible, Torah, and Quran, they could raise a greater sum than is currently pledged by the billionaire Giving Pledge. Is the above arithmetic possible? Of course it is. In fact, Given Pledge adherents will be able to boast nearly a half trillion in cumulative donations over four decades, which will be *in addition to* the $390 billion that is already being donated by American families every year.

Now I can hear some of you saying the billionaires should give more. Fair enough; many of them are leaning on non-pledging billionaires hoping this very thing happens. But remember, this isn't an us versus them exercise. This silent and humble group will have tremendous power to change the world in the way each of them sees fit. In many ways, theirs will be a superior philanthropic model than that of the billionaires.

- They won't have the legal or administrative fees needed to set up a private family foundation as most of their giving will go straight to organizations doing their designated philanthropic work.
- The Given Pledge group's donations will have an immediate impact whereas the billionaires' donations may take decades or centuries to be fully disbursed (private foundations have to distribute only 5% of their assets per year, a practice that is quite common).
- The Given Pledge group won't have to deal with the public scrutiny or judgment that goes along with a more public brand of philanthropy.
- Reporting will be quite simple, ranging from an annual statement included in the family's blessing before the Thanksgiving meal. It might be reported in a letter to family members to be read only after the death of the second spouse. It might just simply be a private, anonymous act of charity known only among the families themselves. Regardless of how it is communicated, it has tremendous and measurable power.

As an added benefit, those who take the pledge will be able to say with clarity that they are wealthy. They are wealthy because they were able to live a wonderful life by living on the 90 cents on the dollar that remains once a tithe is initiated. Are you one of the truly wealthy called to become a member of the Given Pledge?

Let's illustrate what life might look like for a 65-year-old couple who have successfully made "the pledge." They will have the opportunity to draw 4% from their accumulated nest egg, which even at zero growth would allow them an income of $47,000 per year. Added to that we'll assume each member of the couple will qualify for the average social security benefit of $1414 per month, which gives them an additional $33,912 per year. Now what jumps off the page for this modest couple? Their combined income from savings and social security gives them a gross income of $80,912, enough to enjoy the level of happiness and financial security measured by Nobel Prize–winning economist Angus Deaton (we discussed his work in Chap. 3).

This is quite powerful, and brings us back to a few of the people we discussed in Chap. 2. Now, we may envision a couple both of whom decide to become police officers right out of high school. Let's assume one stays on the force through to age 65 without advancing to a higher rank. Let's assume his spouse goes for sergeant after 10 years and that she makes lieutenant after 20 years. Together, the couple will have experienced gross career wages of just over $11 million. They will have begun their tithing at age 25 and have donated nearly $800,000 to charity over their careers. Their nest egg is enough to throw off an income which allows for the maximum amount of measurable happiness stemming from financial security. They won't have one nickel of college debt. This couple, dear readers, is wealthy.

Before you raise your hand in protest or allow yourself to become side-tracked by the inequities we see across our society on a daily basis, consider this: every single one of us who finishes high school and takes the opportunity to learn a trade such as firefighting, policing, plumbing, carpentry, or welding can become wealthy, become philanthropic, and have the opportunity to pursue happiness. This isn't a magic formula for all that ails society, but it is a start. The average Joe has a shot, a very good shot at becoming wealthy and being a real leader and contributor to a better world through his or her philanthropy.

Let's see the Given Pledge (and a savings pledge) take root in our young people before they have made any mistakes. Let's convince them that this is a very real, simple, and repeatable formula. Let's make sure they are aware of this fact before they have signed a lease for a car, before they sign that first apartment lease or mortgage, and before they have a child. Let's remind them that their success, their happiness must come from pride in what they have earned, given, and accomplished rather than how their life compares to their neighbor's or the cover girl on the Robb Report. There aren't enough people going into the classrooms in the inner city schools or in the rural towns reminding kids that success is not a black hole or a closed society. If you are looking for a way to impact society, learn the basics of the Given Pledge and go out and help those kids climb the wall. Don't expect that someone else will do this.

Tell Your Family

Last, but not least, I must once again remind any wealth creator who has or who may establish a large philanthropic program or signed a giving pledge to be certain to tell your family WHY you did it. There are hundreds of billions of dollars sitting in foundations established by now-deceased tycoons whose families have little to no connection to the charity or any understanding about why the foundation even exists. One explanation for this is that these entities lacked a mission statement from the founder, and, more important, there was no word-of-mouth passing down of the family mission through the generations. Remember this: If you feel called to move the needle in the world by giving of your income and your substance, remind your loved ones so that there is someone to take up the mantle after you are gone.

16

Gifting and Estate Planning: Determining the Right Time to Transfer Wealth

There are a number of books that address the various trusts and estate planning structures available to average and wealthy families. In this chapter, I will focus on experiences from families that might help in your own planning. I will also focus on developing a mindset and attitude about the meaning of wealth for your heirs in order to feed the ultimate work ahead in formulating your estate plan.

"I have built such a wonderful life and place for my children to grow up that none of them will ever be able to afford to live here." This was the dilemma a successful Silicon Valley executive shared with me after a recent visit. According to Zillow, in November of 2017, the median home price in Palo Alto, California, was just shy of $3 million. Neighboring communities of Los Altos Hills, Cupertino, and San Francisco came in at $2.8 million, $1.9 million, and $1.5 million, respectively. Silicon Valley real estate was never cheap, but following Facebook's initial public offering with a market capitalization of over $100 million in 2012, what had previously been "paper" internet wealth became real. Many other companies and startups followed in Facebook's wake.

While there were no complaints about this new wealth causing a rising tide for both stock market and real estate prices, there was a dark side to the trend: the communities in which the executives of these companies had established their families had become too expensive for their children to do the same. Many of the newly wealthy executives themselves grew up in much more humble conditions *and* considered the journey from their childhood to Silicon Valley a mark of their success.

© The Author(s) 2019
N. J. Gannon, *Tailored Wealth Management*,
https://doi.org/10.1007/978-3-319-99780-3_16

Now, here's my question: if you believe that the bedrock of financial success lays in a middle-class upbringing and a journey from that place to an institution of higher education, a modest first home, and then a series of jobs that lead to "the big one," is it fair to rob your children of the thrill of that same journey as they stake out their own course in life? Other families might take an opposite (and perfectly reasonable approach) that aims to use the family wealth to dull the sharp edges of life, to allow a younger family member to live in a nicer and safer neighborhood. There is no right or wrong answer to the above dilemma.

The US Marine Corps has a motto, "Every Marine is a rifleman," by which they mean that even as top officers aim for high-ranking Pentagon jobs or as marine aviators, every single officer and enlisted marine will undergo the same tough training, becoming a rifleman, living in the woods with no showers or toilets for weeks at a time, and operating with a constant sleep deficit. Changing that recipe and removing the common bond shared by all marines would be a non-starter.

Similarly, it seems logical that once we identify the raw materials (such as growing up in a middle-class neighborhood, going to a public or neighborhood school, or starting a grass-cutting business at age 13) that led to our own success, we would like to share that knowledge with the next generation in the hope that they will recognize and take advantage of them if and when they are presented.

It also seems obvious that if you have $100 million and enjoy living in one of the most beautiful places on earth that you might want to give each of your children $5 million so they can purchase a home and live close to you. Now ask yourself, will their spouse look at that home with the same pride that you looked at your first home, which you bought after scraping together the 10% down payment? Will they experience the same pride you felt when, after making double mortgage payments, you hit 20% equity for the first time? Will they ever experience the excitement you felt the day you took your final mortgage slip and burned it in the fire pit to celebrate paying it off?

These are important milestones in a person's life and each of us must gauge whether we believe they are necessary for our children's own success or whether our wealth means things should be different for them. A respected colleague, Phil McCauley, CFA, of the Madison Group in Louisville, Kentucky, who falls into the former camp, put his philosophy this way, "I want to leave my children some mountains to climb on their own," in response to my description of the book *100 Places to Take Your Kids Before They Grow Up*.

As I read the book, it struck me that my parents *never* planned to take me to see the Sphinx in Egypt, the Aurora Borealis in Norway, or a breach-ing orca beneath a calving iceberg. The memories I have from childhood include quiet Saturday evenings in front of a roaring fire, watching "The Love Boat" and "Fantasy Island," and eating homemade pizza that my mom prepared. We took one trip to see Niagara Falls and by 2 a.m., after a string of "no vacancy" motel signs, we slept in the car. Six people (including my grandmother) spent that night in our mint green Galaxy 500 two-door. We remember the falls, the trinket stores, and the vivid memory of what it was like to sleep in the car. My children have never spent the night in the car.

Similarly, the issue isn't whether we take our adult children on terrific vacations; it is whether we *should* (if we are wealthy) simply give them the finest things and experiences, even if they are out of their own reach.

Later in our conversation, Phil went on to say, "the pitch of the nose of the plane is more important than the altitude," by which he meant that it is a wonderful thing if each year of our lives could be better than the one that came before it, that each decade could be better than the preceding one, that as we approach each milestone in our lives, we are still growing in terms of our experience, wisdom, generosity, and, also, in our appreciation of the finer things in life.

A balance between giving our children too much and too little can be struck and, in this chapter, I will share some case studies of families that have gotten close to striking it.

The Mathematics of Giving

Gifting to children makes complete mathematical sense, especially if your net worth resides in the shares of a private company that has not reached its potential valuation. It makes perfect mathematical sense to take a married couple's lifetime estate tax exemption ($22.4 million in 2018) and place those funds in a vehicle that will grow OUTSIDE of the donor's estate. Many families wisely gifted their lifetime exemption amount into family trusts in the 1990s and early 2000s. For those that experienced a two- to threefold growth on those assets, that meant the $11 million grew to $22 or $33 million, all of which would be exempt from the estate tax at the death of the senior generation. Once a married couple can reasonably fund the rest of their lives and do anything they wish without tapping into their estate tax exemption, putting it in a trust is worth considering.

Giving Now versus Giving Later

The challenge becomes HOW and WHEN to give your heirs access to the money? Most people agree that handing a $5 million check to a 21-year-old is a bad idea. Many would agree that forcing a trust to distribute income of $100,000 per year at age 21 (as many trusts do) can create a disincentive for the beneficiary to gain meaningful employment. I gained valuable insight into this debate at a meeting of IPI in New York. The interactive session was led by an estate tax attorney and a trust officer. The moderators, requesting a show of hands, asked at what age a child could be given a large financial inheritance or trust distribution WITHOUT it disrupting their lives, career plans, choice of spouse, or character. Age 30? A couple of hands went up. Age 35? About five more hands. Age 40? Eighty percent of the hands in the room went up. This was a fascinating exercise as it was a poll taken among a group that had witnessed wealth transfers occur at a much earlier age and had seen firsthand the benefits and pitfalls that resulted. While it is not a legal term, I have come to describe trusts terms that distribute everything at a certain age or year as a bullet trust.

Pros and Cons of Different Trusts

Most trusts established for young beneficiaries contain language that keeps the assets held in trust up until specified ages, with the trustee having the discretion of making distributions for the health, welfare, and education of the beneficiary. More liberally written documents include the word "lifestyle," which I consider a dangerous addition. The common trust also dictates that at age 21, *income* from the trust is to be distributed to the beneficiary. In these cases, it is common to see two distributions of principal, such as 50% at age 30 and the remainder at age 35 or 40. The income mandate creates a situation where a $10 million trust could create $200,000 in dividend income, even more if the vehicle contained higher-yielding bonds.

The bullet trust contains neither an income mandate nor staggered distributions. On a specified day, such as the 40th birthday of the beneficiary, the trust either makes a full distribution *or* makes the beneficiary a co-trustee in order to "learn the ropes"—in other words, how the trust is managed. Proponents of the standard trust claim that since the child is going to live an upper-class lifestyle anyway, staggering the ages to 21, 30, and 35 gives them the opportunity to learn along the way so that when the trust terminates they will be experienced in managing a large financial asset. There is merit to this claim.

Proponents of the bullet trust value something else: they believe that their children have the right to select their own career path, spouse, city of residence, and place of employment without the financial overlay of a trust, which most certainly will influence their decisions. For this group of clients, I ask, at the time the trust is established, to write a letter to the beneficiary that can be delivered either verbally or in writing if the grantor has passed away. The letter would read something like this:

> Dear son/daughter. Happy 40th Birthday! When you were young, your father and I made a decision to forego a portion of our wealth for your benefit as you grew older. We viewed it as planting a tree that was watered, fertilized, pruned, and protected so that it could grow into something wonderful for you at this stage of your life. You have just turned 40 years old. Your own children may be thinking about college. Precious time on vacation with them will become rarer. You may be considering what your own retirement will look like. The tree has now come into bloom and we hope it will lighten that burden. It may help you send them to a better school. It may help you take a nice vacation. It may allow you to retire a few years earlier. It is now your choice, your tree, and your task to protect. We did this because we love you and at the time we felt it was the wisest decision we could make.
>
> Love, Mom and Dad

This letter may sound completely ridiculous to some and wise in its simplicity to others. The benefit of the bullet trust (and the accompanying letter) is that at all times in the beneficiary's life, the trustee maintains the ability to use trust assets for the health and education of the beneficiary. If the child gets into Harvard and the family is $50,000 short, the trustee can make up the gap. Similarly, if a life-threatening illness strikes the child, the trust can be used for the very best care available. What the trust will NOT fund are swimming pools, BMWs, hot tubs, or drug habits. The right age for the "bloom" of the tree differs among families. They generally select an age at which, they believe, the child will have self-actualized, when the financial benefit of the trust is more likely to help, rather than hurt, him.

There is a downside or criticism to this structure, which is that there are no training wheels since the distribution or co-trusteeship is a single event. Families who choose this structure may have set up smaller Uniform Gifts to Minors Act accounts where their children take control, usually between the ages of 18 and 21, which allows them to learn how to manage their investments, cash flow, and long-term goals. It is critical that I point out that if you have failed to teach your children the lessons of saving, having a work ethic, and delaying gratification (discussed in Part I), the bullet trust could still be damaging to them.

Nota bene: If you choose not to pursue a bullet trust structure, you and your advisor should model a list of scenarios as to what the trust might be worth when income is distributed or at the point(s) where a distribution of principal is authorized. A $10 million trust in 2018 with a 2% yield could produce $200–300,000 in interest and dividends. Only you, as the grantor, can make a determination as to whether this will help or harm your beneficiary.

Pros and Cons of a Simple Wealth Transfer

What about a "traditional" inheritance that happens at the death of the senior generation? It's been around for thousands of years of human history. It still is one of the most popular wealth transfer vehicles even though many millions of dollars are squandered in estate taxes and lost opportunities. Those who prefer to transfer assets at death likely share some thinking in common with the group who prefer bullet trusts. They both want to refrain from financially meddling in the lives of their children. Admittedly, many who choose a simple transfer at death do so because it was too difficult for them to deal with the complexities of lifetime wealth transfer, literally ignoring the job. One obvious drawback to the transfer at death model in our age of longer life expectancy is that one's children might not inherit anything until they were in their late 60s or even 70s if one or both of the spouses see their 90s.

Choosing an Estate Plan That Fits Your Values

There are many complex vehicles; among the most popular are family limited partnerships, grantor retained annuity trusts, charitable remainder trusts, charitable lead annuity trusts, and family insurance trusts. It is critical for a couple not to become bogged down with the legal terms or the buffet of estate and gifting vehicles that are available to them. Rather, they should spend their time discerning the issues of HOW, WHO, and WHEN on a long walk on the beach. These determinations can and should take place over many discussions and be free of the complexities that bog down effective decision-making. Once the couple has figured out what method fits their values, it is time to assemble their financial advisor, accountant, and estate planning attorney to discuss the roadmap. *A word of caution*: If you jump into a plan too early and fund a vehicle before your values have been refined, it is difficult to put the genie back into the bottle.

Of course, the issue of philanthropy comes into play in estate planning. For some, the existence of a defined philanthropic plan is the glue that brings the family together for a common purpose; to do something worthwhile with a portion of the funds from the estate. Billionaires who have signed the Giving Pledge are precise in how they practice this. It is not uncommon for a billionaire to give $100 million each to his three children, and then bequest the remaining $700 million to a charitable foundation. As such a donor sees it, nobody will miss any meals with a $100 million net worth and the act of stewarding the remaining $700 million for the greater good will give purpose to their lives and, for those who need it, will create a counterbalance to the guilt that some feel from being so lucky.

Maintaining Your Estate Plan

An estate plan should be reviewed by your financial advisor and attorney every three to five years. For younger families, reviewing the named guardian for minor children is an important consideration, especially as the children's needs vary. As they become older, an older named guardian's ability to care for them may diminish, so it is important to ensure that you have selected the right person.

The second most important aspect of your estate plan is the naming of a successor trustee. It is important that this individual possesses the skills, temperament, and age that will allow them to faithfully discharge their fiduciary duty on behalf of the beneficiaries. While it may seem obvious, don't neglect ensuring that your named trustee is willing to act in that capacity. You may be surprised to learn how many grantors name a successor trustee without ever asking if they are willing to serve.

Another task that should be performed along with the three- to five-year review is to simply ensure that assets that are supposed to be titled in the name of the trust are correctly titled at the financial institutions that serve as your custodian. It is not at all uncommon for families to go to the trouble of creating a well-thought-out estate plan and then failing to go through the steps of properly titling securities accounts, properties, and bank accounts.

Before You Start, Make Sure You're Clear

The most important thing for a couple to consider is the cause and effect relationship their work and their financial success have had in their own lives and to make a financial plan that does not diminish or hinder the raw materials that drove that success and the pride of self-accomplishment. Only once they have determined what feels right in their gut (including the ability for both spouses to explain in plain English what the purpose of the transfer is intended to accomplish) should they meet with their advisors to discuss strategy and ultimately determine a course of action. This is yet another one of the complex decisions that must be made by families of means in which a slide rule or calculator has limited value.

17

Epilogue

Ron Read, the gas station attendant, was wealthier than gas company (Enron) CEO Ken Lay. There was a cause and effect that led to Read's rise and Lay's fall. We can become wealthier when we recognize our own circumstances on a global scale, then make choices to allocate resources and habits that can feed OUR definition of wealth—whatever that may be.

Managing wealth can be accomplished by filtering out the noise that has led to the complex portfolios that have failed investors over the past two decades. Understanding the relationship between earnings and interest rates is key—remembering that success is always swayed by the price you pay for an asset. The only investment performance that counts over time is that which exists after mistakes, inflation, taxes, and fees.

Composting or redistributing wealth is a necessary and healthy part of the financial ecosystem of our communities and our world. A conscious plan for spending, philanthropy, and legacy for our heirs can and should be a rewarding exercise.

I love to hear when a meat cutter, teacher, or police officer say that they are wealthy—that they have enough. Seek out those who smile as they maximize the resources of their life and situation and ask yourself whether wealth is within your grasp. I believe that it is.

© The Author(s) 2019
N. J. Gannon, *Tailored Wealth Management*,
https://doi.org/10.1007/978-3-319-99780-3_17

Index[1]

---

[1] Note: Page numbers followed by 'n' refer to notes.

© The Author(s) 2019
N. J. Gannon, *Tailored Wealth Management*,
https://doi.org/10.1007/978-3-319-99780-3